STUDIES IN ENGLISH LITERATURE

Volume CVI

X

Scanty Plot of Ground

Studies in the Victorian Sonnet

by

WILLIAM T. GOING
Southern Illinois University at Edwardsville

1976

MOUTON

THE HAGUE - PARIS

ISBN 90 279 3015 5

Printed in the Netherlands

ACKNOWLEDGMENTS

I gratefully acknowledge permission to use material in an earlier form from the following periodicals: on Blunt and Symonds from Victorian Poetry (Spring, 1964 and Spring, 1970), Copyright © West Virginia University, 1964, 1970; on Arnold from Papers on Language and Literature (Fall, 1970), Copyright © Board of Trustees, Southern Illinois University, 1970; on Browning from Tennessee Studies in Literature, Volume XVII, edited by Richard Beale Davis and Kenneth L. Knickerbocker, by permission of The University of Tennessee Press, Copyright © 1972 by The University of Tennessee Press.

I am indebted to Southern Illinois University at Edwardsville for research grants-in-aid and for a two-quarter sabbatical that made parts of this research possible.

For help and advice at all stages of the preparation of these essays, I am grateful to my wife, Margaret Moorer Going, who is in her own right a scholar of British literature.

W. T. G.
Edwardsville, Illinois
1974

CONTENTS

PREFACE

In 1827 when Wordsworth warned critics to "scorn not the Sonnet", he would scarcely have believed how seriously nineteenth-century poets would take his suggestion. Leading the way with well over five hundred sonnets, he himself could not be accused of writing "alas, too few" as he had accused Milton. "Twas pastime to be bound/Within the Sonnet's scanty plot of ground", Wordsworth had declared earlier; the Victorians believed that he was right, and they set about emulating his example.

This series of essays, however, does not constitute a history of that Victorian sonnet emulation, nor is it a detailed account of the impact of the sonnets of other Romantic poets, almost all of whom made remarkable contributions to the genre. Those works remain to be written.

The present group of studies is a series of essays selectively illuminating, it is hoped, some of the highpoints in sonneteering after 1830. The emphasis here falls on the sonnet sequence, itself a Victorian term, because the age was the most prolific time of sonnet series; the appendix lists almost 4000 sonnets in some 230 Victorian sequences—a list that could be greatly expanded among other minor poets. Like the great series of the English Renaissance, Sonnets from the Portuguese, Modern Love, The House of Life, and Monna Innominata are preeminent works; and the poetic reputations of Mrs. Browning, Meredith, the Rossettis, Hopkins, Blunt, Symonds, and Bridges rest to a large extent on their sonnet sequences. To put the matter still another way, the major Victorian poets— Tennyson, Browning, Arnold, the Rossettis, Meredith, Hopkins, Swinburne, and Hardy— all wrote sonnet sequences.

By offering the essays somewhat chronologically and beginning with a historical-critical essay on the nature of the Victorian sequence, this study attempts to single out significant aspects of sonneteering among the three generations of Victorian poets— from the dramatically ironic attitude of Browning, to an examination of the whole body of Arnold's single sonnets, to the fin de siècle efforts of Wilfrid Scawen Blunt and John Addington Symonds.

1. THE NATURE OF THE VICTORIAN SONNET SEQUENCE

(A)

For almost four centuries both the sonnet and the sonnet sequence
have been significant genres in English poetry. During the
Elizabethan age and the nineteenth century they were especially
popular with major poets, minor poets and poetasters. The history of the Elizabethan sonnet sequence has been rather carefully examined; almost every account of the sonnet during the
Renaissance in England is in reality an account of the sonnet
sequence. But the history of the sonnet as well as that of the
sonnet sequence during the nineteenth century has yet to be
written. For the nineteenth century belongs to the recent past;
the number of sonnets, sonneteers, and publishing and printing
establishments is far greater in the nineteenth century; the sonnet and the sonnet sequence have become after Milton's insistence on the single sonnet two distinct genres; and the scope of
subject matter and conventions of technique for the sonnet as
well as for the sonnet sequence during the Romantic and Victorian periods have become broader and more varied and hence
more complicated to analyze and describe.

In a consideration of representative Victorian sonnet sequences
certain characteristics of sonnet groupings prior to 1830 are
pertinent. Two salient facts about Elizabethan sonnet cycles are
these: almost all of any importance were written in the last decade of the sixteenth century; almost all were concerned with love
after the manner of "Petrarch's long deceased woes". Although
the sonnets of neither Wyatt nor Surrey can be said to form a
series except in the sense that they were printed in Tottel's
Songes and Sonnettes of 1557 one after the other, these sonnets
by being consecutively grouped in imitation of the Italian collections became seeds of the great harvest of Petrarchan series
that was to follow a quarter of a century later. In 1591 Sidney's
Astrophel and Stella brought the form to fruition; then followed
the collections of Barnes, Daniel, Constable, Lodge, and Drayton.
After Spenser's Amoretti in 1595, as Janet Scott has demonstrated,
the sonnet fell into the hands of rimers like Griffin, Linche, and
Smith to disappear in the ridicule cast on the form by writers of

epigrams and satire. (1) Shakespeare's sonnets, though written chiefly before 1600, appeared much later. And the sonnets of Drummond of Hawthornden, which appeared still later, were in style and spirit a part of this sixteenth-century English vogue.

When the Elizabethan sequences are examined as sequences, they are usually found wanting in unity, either thematic or organic. Drayton, for instance, in Ideas Mirrour, writing in general terms on topics like celestial numbers, imagination, folly, and the soul, seems to ignore constantly, as Sir Sidney Lee has shown, the lady to whom he professes to owe his inspiration. (2) The majority of sonnets in even the best cycles — those of Sidney, Shakespeare, and Spenser — can be transposed at will without doing the cycles much damage. In the whole of these sequences only here and there does a sonnet really depend for its thought and meaning upon anything that has gone before. Yet it is the proof of the genius of these three poets that within the conventional Petrarchan patterns of the Italian and French poets whom they imitated and frequently translated they were able to suggest an underlying autobiographical thread of narration. But the slight unity of the cycles was that of mood rather than event; their power lay in individual sonnets rather than in the cycles as wholes

A second point about the unity of the Elizabethan sequences is that they were less likely to include prose and verses in various lyric patterns than were Italian and French cycles. Occasionally, to gain a closer unity, poets as different as Gascoigne and Donne employed artificial linking devices. Gascoigne in a "sequence" of three sonnets in "Weeds" begins the second with the additional short line "For Lucius he", and the third sonnet similarly begins with the rhyming epigraph "But Fotis she". Donne in La Corona forms a linked wreath of seven sonnets, as the Italian poet Caro had done, with the last line of each repeated as the opening line of the following (and with the first line of the first sonnet being the last line of the last). In the main, the subject matter of the Elizabethan cycles was conventions of courtly love, but other matter was not totally excluded. Barnes and Constable each wrote collections of "Spirituall Sonnets", Henry Lok published in 1597 a group of 328 Sundrie Sonnets of Christian Passions, with other Affectionate Sonnets of a Feeling Conscience Chapman composed a series of philosophical sonnets; Sir John Davies, a group of satirical sonnets; and John Donne, in addition to La Corona, wrote a deeply passionate series of Holy Sonnets after the death of his wife. Thus the tendency to broaden the subject matter of the sonnet sequence is evident in the midst of the fashionable, imitative mania of writing sonnets about the beauties and cruelties of a mistress. Although the methods of unifying most of the sequences were haphazard, at least Sydney, Shakespeare, and Spenser suggested the possibility of making the sonnet sequence an artistic and subtle autobiographic confessional even within the conventional Petrarchan framework of conceits. And ingenious craftsmen, like Gascoigne at the beginning of the period and Donne at the end, called attention to exterior motifs for linking sonnets in sequence.

In addition to the sonnets of Drummond of Hawthornden and John Donne, which really belong to the Elizabethan age of sonnieteering, the great name in the seventeenth century was Milton. In the history of the sonnet sequence Milton is unique: his influence was dominant in the late eighteenth and early nineteenth-century sequences, yet he himself wrote no sequence unless his Italian sonnets are so considered. In fact, after the opening decades of the seventeenth century sequences were seldom written. (3) Moreover, from 1645 to 1700 there appeared in print only 153 original sonnets, including those of Milton. By the late seventeenth century, the sonnet was largely forgotten. (4) In 1687 Philip Ayres prefaced his sonnets with this doubtful recommendation:

> None of our great men, either Mr. Waller, Mr. Cowley, or Mr. Dryden. . . have ever stooped to anything of this sort . . . Many eminent persons have published several things of this nature . . . as the famous Mr. Spencer, Sir Philip Sidney, Sir Richard Fanshawe, Mr. Milton and some few others. The success of all which in these things, I must needs say, cannot much be boasted of.

This same attitude of scorn and lack of understanding of the sonnet carried over into the beginning of the eighteenth century. When John Hughes edited the works of Spenser in 1715, he stated in the preface:

> I shall . . . say something of the Sonnets, a Species of Poetry so entirely disus'd, that it seems to be scarce known among us at this time . . . The Sonnet consists generally of one Thought, and that always turn'd in a single Stanza, of fourteen Lines, of the Lengths of our

Heroicks, the Rhimes being interchanged alternately
. . . . Milton has writ some, both in <u>Italian</u> and English,
and is, I think, the last who has given us any Example of
them in our own Language.

Even though some three thousand sonnets were published between
1700 and 1800, Professor Havens believed that hardly more than
thirty deserve to live. (5) The leading poets of the century wrote
almost no sonnets; they apparently felt with Dr. Johnson that sonneteering was a pastime for dilettantes — a matter of carving
"heads upon cherry stones", even Milton's sonnets being "those
little pieces [to] be dispatched without much anxiety". In this in-
hospitable atmosphere it is not surprising that the eighteenth century produced no sonnet sequences of any serious poetic merit.
In the two closing decades of the century, however, when single
sonnets by Bampfylde, the Wartons, Bowles, and others were
being read with interest, the sonnet sequence was revived. The
<u>Lady's Poetical Magazine</u> of 1781 printed posthumously the series
<u>Death</u> by Charles Emily, who continued the tradition of Donne's
<u>Holy Sonnets</u> in the vogue of Young and Blair. But it was probably
Edmund Cartwright "who first stumbled upon a new sort of sequence, which was characterized by independence of theme and
treatment. Its unity was achieved by a dominant idea, philosophical, political, or personal, of which each sonnet was one facet,
quite independent of the others". (6) In <u>Sonnets to Eminent Men</u>
(1783) Cartwright praised the achievements of William Jones,
William Hayley, Thomas Warton, Richard Watson, Thomas
Thurlow, and Charles Lennox. A decade later Coleridge used the
same tradition in <u>Sonnets on Eminent Characters</u> when he honored
Thomas Erskine, Burke, Priestley, La Fayette, Kosciuszko,
Bowles, Mrs. Siddons, Godwin, Southey, Sheridan, and Lord
Stanhope, and condemned Pitt with bitter scorn and irony. In sim-
lar vein the 1797 edition of Southey's <u>Poems</u> contained a series of
six sonnets on the slave trade:

> . . . I do feel upon my cheek the glow
> Of indignation when beneath the rod
> A sable brother writhes in silent woe.

In the same year Charles Lamb and Charles Lloyd wrote loosely
connected sonnets about their relatives. Thus in the closing year
of the eighteenth century a new tradition of sonnet sequences,

growing out of the subject matter and spirit of Milton's single sonnets, was being molded. Here was a medium in which a poet could meditate, praise, condemn, or simply describe the world about him and his feeling toward it in short poems joined together by unity of theme and title.

The amatory sequence, however, was not entirely dead in these years, for in 1789 an unknown "Benedict" wrote ten sonnets to "Melissa" in The World, and in 1796 Mrs. Mary Robinson, a protégé of Garrick and a friend of Reynolds, Godwin, and Coleridge (who wrote a sonnet to her), published a series of forty-four sonnets Sappho and Phaon. Mrs. Robinson wrote under a semi-allegoric guise about her desertion by her lover, the Prince of Wales, later George IV, employing the familiar Petrarchan conventions in the elaborate diction of the Della Cruscan school.

Though almost no one would suggest that the sonnet sequences of the closing years of the eighteenth century were significant poetry, the prototypes of some of the main traditions of the nineteenth-century sequence were making their appearance: the amatory tradition of Mrs. Robinson and the descriptive-meditative tradition of Emily, Cartwright, Coleridge and Southey.

(B)

In the representative list of English sonnet sequences of the eighteenth and nineteenth centuries in the Appendix, upon which this discussion is based, there are only eleven sequences listed between 1700 and 1800, and over 250 between 1800 and 1900. (7) These figures are even more indicative of a trend when one realizes that further research will reveal few more seventeenth or eighteenth-century sequences, while many more nineteenth-century ones—particularly by minor poets—will undoubtedly come to light. (8) Furthermore, since only twenty-seven (excluding translations) of these 250 were published before 1830, it may be said that the most prolific period of the sonnet sequence was the Victorian (although the most prolific decade of the sonnet sequence was that from 1591 to 1599). The amatory and the descriptive-meditative are the two dominant traditions of the nineteenth-century sonnet sequence; and these traditions can best be examined from three points of view: the subject matter of the sequences, the methods of linking sonnets in sequences, and the originality and consequent influence of certain seminal sequences. (9)

The traditions of subject matter can most easily be analyzed in the table on page 16 based on the list of sequences in the Appendix. Even though due allowance is made for the fallacy of such rigid, unqualified grouping and for the sampling technique, certain trends are markedly evident. The amatory tradition, which had died in ridicule at the end of the sixteenth century, again came into favor among the Victorians. Between the end of the English Renaissance and 1850 there were few amorous sequences: Mrs. Robinson's <u>Sappho and Phaon</u> is the only one of any length. And to its credit, despite mannered diction and Della Cruscan artificialities, the sonnets follow the Petrarchan patterns. Mrs. Robinson did not write the popular loose elegiac quatorzains like those of Mrs. Charlotte Smith which attracted the youthful Coleridge to describe the form as requiring "some lonely feeling" with "rhymes, many or few, or no rhymes at all".

A shorter series was Keats's 1817 group of three sonnets, "Woman, when I behold thee flippant, vain". Though not among his best sonnets, the triad, probably written under the influence of Leigh Hunt, is interesting in its theme of love and chivalric reverence for woman and as evidence of Keats's search for a larger lyric stanzaic pattern than the single sonnet. Aside from Lamb's "ewe lambs" to Ann Simmons, William Curtis's backward-looking <u>Amoretti</u>, and Tennyson's and Hallam's then unknown short sequences, the only other widely known amorous series before 1850 was a group of eleven Shakespearean sonnets in Disraeli's <u>Venetia</u> (1837). This popular novel records a highly fictionalized account of the lives of Shelley and Byron, both of whom write sonnet sequences to their loves before sharing a common grave in the Gulf of Spezzia. In the novel the sequence of Marmion Herbert (Shelley) is referred to but not reproduced; that of Lord Cadurcis (Byron) to Venetia (Herbert's daughter by his estranged wife) is reproduced in full. The style is a heavy-handed imitation of Byron:

Strange were his musing thoughts and trembling heart,
'Tis strange they met, and stranger if they part.
. . . like Cain, he wandered forth to roam.

If not as sonnets, the poem is interesting as a sequence, for as Cadurcis recounts his life of "orphan lord" to Herbert's daughter

SUBJECT MATTER OF REPRESENTATIVE SONNET SEQUENCES 1781(a) – 1900(b)

Subject Matter	1781 – 1830		1831 – 1900	
	Number of Sequences	Number of Sonnets in Sequences	Number of Sequences	Number of Sonnets in Sequences
Love	7	105	36	795
Nature & Place	6	115	76	1409
Religion	2	173	28	706
History & Politics	8	24	28	436
Literature & Criticism	3	28	21	171
Death & Commemoration	3	35	21	144
Personal Life & Philosophy	6	29	24	601
	30	509	234	4262

(a) Date of earliest known eighteenth century sonnet sequence.
(b) A few of the sequences of Victorian poets appeared after 1900.

"of a noble race", the series takes on a narrative quality that anticipates the later work of Meredith and Symonds. Like <u>Modern Love</u> and <u>Stella Maris</u> some of the sonnets are not entirely detachable as clearly understandable poems in their own right, and the opening lines of several begin with such transitional terms as <u>For</u> and <u>Thus</u>:

> For, from his ancient home, a scatterling
> They drove him . . . (V)

> Thus she also knows the orphan role. (VI)

> My tale is done . . . (XI)

If the Romantic poets neglected to write amorous sonnet sequences, Disraeli and his avid Victorian readers felt that the neglect should be remedied.

It was not, however, until 1850 that the nineteenth century produced a series of love sonnets worthy of being placed beside the great Elizabethan cycles. Despite the quantity of material written about <u>Sonnets from the Portuguese</u>, there have been almost no explanations as to why Miss Barrett selected this particular genre. That she knew the Elizabethan sequences and the series of Wordsworth is no real explanation. It is probably more significant that her 1844 <u>Poems</u> contained twenty-eight sonnets. Of these, two are of special interest: "To George Sand. A Desire" and "To George Sand. A Recognition". They form a connected pair concerned with the theme of one whose nature is both "large-brained woman and large-hearted man". To deny the true woman in the true genius is "vain denial". Shortly thereafter when Robert Browning sent his letters of love and finally made his appearance at Wimpole Street, Elizabeth was face-to-face with such a crisis. She recorded her emotions and doubts and final capitulation in letters and in sonnets that closely resemble each other in mood, thought and feeling. The denial of the woman for the hypochondriac daughter and the popular poetess was "vain denial".

In the summer of 1846 Miss Barrett bought for 2s. 6d. a notebook into which she copied with many corrections the now-familiar sonnets, the last being dated "1846, Sept.", the month of marriage. It seems reasonable to suppose, then, that this significant landmark in the development of the sonnet sequence

grew naturally and spontaneously into the unique work that it is:
a sonnet record of the crystallized moments of Miss Barrett's
joy, doubt, and hope in being wooed by him of the "princely
heart".

Sonnets from the Portuguese is, moreover, a unique norm
for the amatory sequence. The outline of the underlying narrative is clear and simple: there is no doubt about the "off-stage
story" as there is in Shakespeare's sonnets. The series is not
discursive and inclusive like those of Petrarch and Drayton. It
has unity of theme; it has beginning, climax (Sonnet XVI "Here
ends my strife"), denouement, and conclusion (Sonnet XLIII "I
shall but love thee better after death"). The individual sonnets
are detachable poems, clearly separate entities, which are
nevertheless more meaningful when read in sequence. Some of
the sonnets may be transposed, but not so many as in the
Elizabethan cycles or in The House of Life. Yet unlike many of
the individual poems of Modern Love almost none of the
Portuguese Sonnets depends upon a preceding one for its
immediate and full comprehension.

The sonnets gain a further unity by the repetition of certain
recurrent images. The lover is referred to as a "princely
heart", one who has his "calling to some palace floor", "a
princely giver", and "noble and like a king". And purple, the
color of royalty, occurs in Sonnets VII, IX, XVI. The figure of
life compared to a garment is echoed in Sonnet XII from Sonnet
VIII. The Love-not-Death motif may be found in Sonnets I, VII,
XVIII, XXXIX and XLII. And finally, there is also a certain
unity of effect gained by employing the identical rime-scheme
in every sonnet of the sequence.

It is customary to find fault with Mrs. Browning's diction,
turbidity of movement, generality of figure, and careless rimes.
However that may be, the significance of Sonnets from the
Portuguese, first published at the midpoint of the century, cannot
be overemphasized in any account, however brief, of the sonnet
sequence in English.

Between the work of Mrs. Browning and Modern Love in 1862,
the only significant amatory series is a group of seven Undergraduate Sonnets (unpublished during his lifetime) by the youthful
Swinburne; in lilting measure these sonnets imitate the
Elizabethan love conventions and exaggerate in peculiarly
Swinburnian fashion the cruelty of a mistress. Far from imitative,
however, are the fifty sonnets of Meredith's Modern Love. In

fact, the Elizabethan convention of writing a sonnet to one's mistress's eyes is cruelly satirized in Sonnet XXX, where the husband reminds the new "Lady", whom he sets out to win for distraction's sake, that we human beings are intelligences with predatory animal instincts: "Lady, this is my sonnet to your eyes". Although Ann Bannerman in her 1800 Sonnets from "Werter" (which Meredith probably never knew) anticipates his method of dramatizing high points in a story, Meredith in Modern Love reflects in sonnet glimpses a partly fictional and partly autobiographic account of the tragedy of his first marriage.

As a whole, Modern Love is more complex than Mrs. Browning' sequence. Instead of the usual two characters there are four; instead of a single point of view Modern Love reflects the points of view of three of the four characters. The key to Meredith's structure and linking devices is the awareness of a lyric medium that gives the subtle accumulative effect of a narrative one. Certain sonnets can be moved about in position, though far fewer than in Sonnets from the Portuguese, and yet there are few prosy links in the midst of lyric poems as there are, for instance, in John Addington Symonds' Stella Maris (1884). In attempting to work in the same narrative-amatory tradition Symonds resorts to notes explanatory of the "story" and to such straight narrative lines as "It came at length, our meeting" (XXXV), "and then she rose" (XXXVIII). "She then is flown" (XLVII), "they write me, Stella, write me thou are mad" (LII). Meredith is much more subtle. The characters, for instance, are unnamed: the husband is "I"-and-"he", the wife's lover is "the man", the wife is "Madam", and the husband's love is "My Lady". The effect is to some extent the tragedy of every husband and wife caught in a loveless marriage. The reader is not precisely told in expository links that the final attempt at reconciliation between the husband and wife has failed; this fact is implied in the descriptive image:

> Mark where the pressing wind shoots javelin-like,
> Its skeleton shadow on the broad-backed wave!
> Here is a fitting spot to dig Love's grave.

Modern Love has often been compared to a "naked novel" in fifty chapters. But if so, it is a novel by an author who Oscar Wilde said could do everything but tell a story. The sonnet-chapters are momentary glimpses and reflections on the bitter life of the

poet-husband and his wife. These two play at <u>Hiding the Skeleton</u>
when they have guests for dinner. They walk through their garden
tortured with private memories while Madam speaks scandal of
old friends. When she is in a mood for reconciliation, he freezes
her with commonplaces. The poem is thus a sequence of
emotional reflections which produce the effect of a novel un-
folded in dramatic scenes.

The third important archetype of the amatory tradition in the
nineteenth-century sonnet sequence is Rossetti's <u>The House of
Life</u>. Of the three it was perhaps the most influential among the
poets of the century, probably because of the dynamic charm of
the man and a worshipful, imitative coterie of poets and critics
who admired the growth of the work. At the time of a renewed
interest in the Renaissance, Rossetti's loose organization —
almost a sort of <u>omnium gatherum</u> about love — suggested the
charm of Petrarch's Laura and the mystery of Shakespeare's
Dark Lady. The number of sonnets and the text of <u>Sonnets from
the Portuguese</u> and <u>Modern Love</u> have remained almost unchanged from their first publication, but <u>The House of Life</u> has
had a long history of addition and subtraction from the 1869
publication of "Sonnets and Songs toward a Work to be called 'The
House of Life'" to William Michael Rossetti's restoration of the
notorious "Nuptial Sleep" in the illustrated edition of 1904. Like
Whitman's <u>Leaves of Grass</u> these expanding editions — along with
rumors of exhuming MSS. from a dead wife's grave and the bitter
attacks on Rossetti's moral character by the angry Scotch re-
viewer Buchanan, who also wrote sonnet sequences but in the
Wordsworthian manner — kept the title before the public. <u>The
House of Life</u> thus became

> the House of Rossetti's life during his most vital years
> of poetic composition and emotional intensity, his struggle
> with the baffling mysteries of life and love and death
> . . . yet those who have sought a particular arrangement
> or coherence in the series have come away with disap-
> pointing results; even the clues which Rossetti gave in the
> captions, 'Part I. Youth and Change', 'Part II. Change and
> Fate', are not very helpful. (10)

It is precisely this lack of apparent coherence in Rossetti's poem
that makes it somewhat uninteresting as a sonnet sequence — but
not as a group of sonnets. The unity is the unity of its theme —

ramifications of sensual and spiritual love—and the unity of
mood and language in describing his love for Lizzie Siddal,
Alexa Wilding, Fanny Cornforth, and Jane Burden Morris. Here
is no narrative of a single crisis or psychological development
which is found, in varying measure, in the sequences of Mrs.
Browning and Meredith. The beauty and power of The House of
Life lies in the fundamental brainwork of the imagery and idea,
which, deriving from personal experience, are transmuted into
ideal and generalized concepts.

The year 1881 saw the publication of The House of Life in its
expanded form of 102 sonnets as well as the publication of two
sequences by Christina Rossetti—Monna Innominata and Later
Life. The former, a series of fourteen, traces the emotional
impact of the poet's love for a nameless loved one, perhaps
either the scholar and translator Charles Cayley or the Scottish
poet, William Bell Scott. Like Mrs. Browning, whom she called
"Great poetess of our own day and nation", Christina writes of
the influence of love, but her tone is sad and sombre, and her
point of view is retrospective. Like the Sonnets from the
Portuguese the title Monna Innominata (one of the nameless
Italian ladies beloved of poets like Dante and Petrarch, as is
explained in Christina's headnote) is in William Michael's phrase
"a blind intended to draw off attention from the writer in her
proper person"; and also like the Sonnets from the Portuguese
the sequence has simple structure, the climax coming in the
opening of Sonnet IX:

> Thinking of you, and all that was, and all
> That might have been and now can never be . . .

The opening moods of joy and pain have given way to renunciation
followed by the Christian consolation that in the second life all is
love. This donna innominata would commend her earthly lover,
whose faith does not match hers, to God, "Whose love your love
capacity can fill".

Interesting to note in Monna Innominata is the subtitle "A
Sonnet of Sonnets": fourteen lines—fourteen sonnets; the volta
of the sonnet after the eighth line—the volta of the sequence
after the eighth sonnet. Of the superficial methods for linking
sonnets in sequence this is surely one of the neatest prosodic
devices. On the other hand, Later Life: A Double Sonnet of
Sonnets has neither organic nor thematic unity. Christina

Rossetti's shorter sequences, <u>They Desire a Better Country</u> and <u>By Way of Remembrance</u>, have some of the unity of mood and underlying thread of story of <u>Monna Innominata</u> as well as the matchless simplicity of her sonnet technique that came from a lifetime of practice—beginning with the childhood game of "bouts rimés", played with Dante Gabriel.

The sequence most closely agreeing with Christina's in its philosophy of love is Robert Bridges' <u>Growth of Love</u>, where love is, as Professor Guérard says, "a spiritual discipline for the individual in his progress toward perfection". (11) Like <u>The House of Life</u> Bridges' sequence had a long history of growth and change — of addition, subtraction, and re-writing of sonnets; and like Rossetti's, Bridges' work has little organic unity, although parts have impressive beauty of sustained mood. The unifying <u>motif</u> here is that of style and of implied philosophy. The purity and power of the diction suggest the Elizabethan sonneteers at their best; the philosophy attempts to suggest a relationship of all-inclusive love and beauty as a way of salvation for rational man.

The remaining amatory sequences, though some contain distinguished individual sonnets, are less important works in comparison with the cycles of Mrs. Browning, Meredith, the Rossettis, and Bridges. Philip Bourke Marston, the blind poet, follows the loose organization of his friend Rossetti in his long sequence in <u>Songtide</u>, celebrating his love for Mary Nesbit, and in the shorter <u>Preludes</u>, recounting his emotions after her death. Also in the pattern of Rossetti's sequence are William Sharp's <u>Sonnet-Sequence</u>, a series of emotional reflections on love once fulfilled only to be terminated by death, William Bell Scott's <u>Outside the Temple</u> and <u>Parted Love</u>, and Ernest Dowson's <u>Sonnets of a Little Girl</u>, which is unified by its melancholy tone and its image of a tender, grey-eyed child, whose

Love alone is stingless and can calm
Life's fitful fever with its healing balm . . . .

Let us go hence: the night is now at hand.

And at the end of the century Lord Alfred Douglas was still writing sonnets <u>To Olive</u> in this same tradition:

When I am dead you shall not doubt or fear,

And I, in the dark ante-room of Death,
Will wait for you with ever-outstretched hands . . .
my arms will be like bands
And all my weakness like your winding-sheet.

Along with this attitude of decadence toward which Pre-
Raphaelitism led, there grew up a counter-movement of
"natural life", usually portrayed in the more compact structure
of the narrative-amatory tradition of Modern Love. Such a poem
is the short sequence of Thomas Hardy, She to Him, which tells
in dramatic glimpses of a man's cruel treatment of a woman who
has lost her beauty and thereby all her physical attraction for
him. In this same spirit is Hopkins' The Beginning of the End.
The influence of Meredith, whose Modern Love he had read, is
apparent in the opening sonnet of this early and probably unfinished series:

You see that I have come to passion's end;
This means you need not fear the storms, the cries,
That gave you vantage when you would despise:
My bankrupt heart has no more tears to spend.

And the tradition of Mrs. Browning's sequence—that of a happy
human love told in emotional glimpses, implying an underlying
narrative—also had its followers. Edmund Gosse's Fortunate
Love, Sir William Watson's Sonnets to Miranda, and Francis
Thompson's Ad Amicam are examples.

In the latter part of the nineteenth century, then, the amatory
is again a well-reëstablished type of sequence. Its subject
matter is varied: human passion and self-fulfillment may lead to
misery or to happiness, or they may be sublimated into sacred
or ideal love. Bridges, beginning his sonnets with the Petrarchan
love conventions, writes of a love revealed in the smile of one
lady and in all forms of earthly beauty, finally leading to a
Platonic Eternal Beauty. With Christina Rossetti human and
divine love are complementary:

I cannot love you if I love not Him,
I cannot love Him if I love not you.

She can never, like Mrs. Browning, exchange her "near sweet
view of Heaven" for the noble human love of one mortal man.

Dante Gabriel blends in well-wrought harmony the fleshly and spiritual aspects of love. Symonds, disillusioned with his Venetian love, Stella, seeks an ideal love, "Love's Self", while Meredith and Hardy make "a dissection of the sentimental passion of these days". Ernest Dowson would entwine his hand in that of a tender child who should never grow up, and Gerard Manley Hopkins after "all passion spent" finds the dominant of his passion: "Love, O my God, to call Thee Love and Love". And the sequences of Wilfrid Blunt—Love Sonnets of Proteus, Esther, and Natalia's Resurrection—are representative of the gamut of themes and structures in the amatory tradition.

The methods of unifying love sonnets into sequences fall chiefly into two traditions: the lyric-amatory and the narrative-amatory. In the former category Sonnets from the Portuguese and The House of Life are the archetypes. Mrs. Browning's sequence centers the sonnets around one episode and thereby suggests an underlying thread of "story" in lyrics climatically arranged, while Rossetti's is an anthology of lyrics reflecting many episodes thematically arranged according to the gamut of lyric emotions. In the narrative-amatory tradition Modern Love is the archetype. By delineating character and implying scene Meredith's sequence suggests in sharply pointed lyrics the effect of narration.

(C)

The subject matter (see chart on page 16), however, makes quite evident the fact that love is by no means the only subject of the nineteenth-century sonnet sequence: nature and place, religion, history and politics, literature and criticism, death and commemoration, personal life and philosophy. In short, just as the subject matter of the sonnet has been broadened from its first and dominant matter of love, so has the sonnet sequence experienced a similar broadening scope. What is subject matter for one sonnet is likewise fitting for a pair and hence for groups of three or more.

In the preface to the 1815 edition of his poems Wordsworth states that the "materials of Poetry . . . are cast by means of various moulds into diverse forms". These he lists as: 1. Narrative (containing the epopoeia, tale, romance, etc.), 2. Dramatic (including tragedy, comedy, masque, opera, etc.), 3. Lyrical (including hymn, ode, elegy, the song, etc.),

4. Idyllium ("Descriptive chiefly either of the processes and
appearances of external nature . . . The Epitaph, the Inscription,
the Sonnet, most of the Epistles of poets writing in their own
persons, and all loco-descriptive poetry, belong to this class
. . . .") To Wordsworth, then, at the opening of the nineteenth
century, the sonnet was a descriptive-meditative vehicle concerned with nature and place, and before the end of his long
career he would have added history and politics, religion,
literature and criticism, personal life and philosophy, for he
composed not only sonnets but sonnet sequences on aspects of
all these subjects. Among the major poets during the first half
of the century Wordsworth was the most important composer of
series of sonnets, and his work furnished the archetypes for the
meditative-descriptive tradition. (12)

That Wordsworth should think of the sonnet as a descriptive
and didactic medium is not surprising. He learned his sonnet
craftmanship from Milton. The eighteenth-century sonneteers
(whom Wordsworth knew well) were also heavily indebted to
Milton; and Bampfylde, the Wartons, Bowles, Mrs. Smith, and
others had already established a tradition of writing of the
"beauties of nature" in the sonnet "mould". But the sonnet sequence Wordsworth seems to have re-discovered for himself.
In 1820 he published The River Duddon: A Series of Sonnets,
and this provided the archetype for the descriptive-meditative
(or what Wordsworth calls the "loco-descriptive") tradition of
the sonnet sequence. There was nothing startlingly new about
the subject matter. Bowles among others had already written
sonnets about rivers; in a footnote to his introduction to the
1837 edition of his poems, he writes about his early sonnets:
"The subjects were chiefly from river scenery . . . they were
published ten years before those of Mr. Wordsworth on the
river Duddon, Yarrow, et cet." Wordsworth's contribution, in
addition to his special way of combining natural description
with personal philosophy, was his method of linking the sonnets
in series—precisely what Bowles lacked in his Fourteen Sonnets.
The plan is a simple geographical one: the Duddon from source
to sea—with the usual digressions. Wordsworth describes with
minute care the cloud-born source of the stream, the flowers,
trees, and cottages along its nursling course, the stepping-stones
that lead across it, and the rustic bridge that arches its widened
expanse. After pausing to recall such digressive matters as
American Indian legends about the Oroonoko river, he traces the

Duddon to the sea; but the partner of his youth is not entirely
gone — it remains a symbol for all nature which "was, and is,
and will abide". The memory of the Duddon makes us "feel
that we are greater than we know".

The only other group of nature sonnets before Wordsworth's
in 1820 that might be called a series are Leigh Hunt's sonnets
To Hampstead, which were first published in The Examiner
from 1813 to 1815. Collected into his 1815 poems, the sonnets
do not actually have an over-all title, the first being called "To
Hampstead" and the other four "To the Same", and one which
was entitled "Hampstead VII" was not reprinted until 1818, when
it had a separate title "Description of Hampstead". That Leigh
Hunt proposed a sort of grouping is evident from his numbering —
or rather, his misnumbering — in The Examiner, but that the
sonnets have any particular order or are related except by theme
and style is not apparent.

With Wordsworth's publication of Poems Composed or
Suggested during a Tour in the Summer of 1833 and Yarrow
Revisited in 1835 (13) a slightly different type of sequence was
introduced: the tour sequence. The method of unifying the sonnets
is merely that of the itinerary, but this slight framework provides an ordered means for describing nature and place and
thoughts along the way about "steamboats, viaducts, and rail-
ways". In the 1830's Wordsworth's pattern of grouping descriptive
sonnets in series began to be widely imitated. Throughout the rest
of the century, poets — particularly minor poets — poured forth
their sonnet effusions. After Wordsworth, the deluge.
Mrs. Hemans writes her Records of the Autumn of 1834 and
Records of the Spring of 1834, Ebenezer Elliott records his
Rhymed Rambles in forty-seven sonnets, and Sir Aubrey de Vere,
one of Wordsworth's acknowledged disciples, describes Atlantic
Coast Scenery, and his son Aubrey Thomas, the landmarks of
Europe, particularly Italy. The magazines capitalized on des-
criptions of the grandeur of nature, particularly of far-off places:
from May, 1844 to June, 1845 Tait's Edinburgh Magazine pub-
lished in installments seventy-eight anonymous sonnets entitled
A Rosary from the Rhine. Even the rather cumbersome titles of
Wordsworth's series were imitated: David Macbeth Moir's
Sonnets on the Scenery of the Esk and Sonnets on the Scenery of
the Tweed, Catherine Godwin's Four Sonnets Written during a
Summer Tour on the Continent, and Frederick Faber's Memorials of a Happy Time. And even Rossetti's Scotch antagonist

Buchanan indulged in thirty-four <u>Sonnets Written by Loch Coruisk</u>.
Not all of these writers were mere poetasters; the three
usually acknowledged best sonneteers of the early Victorian
period — all followers of Wordsworth — composed sequences of
this sort: Charles Tennyson Turner's <u>Great Localities: An
Inspiration</u>, Aubrey Thomas de Vere's <u>Urbs Roma</u>, and Hartley
Coleridge's <u>Sonnets Suggested by the Seasons</u>. At the end of the
century the genre was losing its appeal, but John Addington
Symonds was still describing the Swiss scenery around Davos;
and Watts-Dunton, the countryside between Jowett's home and
Oxford — <u>The Last Walk from Boar's Hill</u>.
In his study of the early Victorian sonnet, Professor Sanderlin
states that "after 1839 the religious sonnet displaced the descriptive as the most popular type". (14) Such was also the case with
the sonnet sequence. And it was Wordsworth again who furnished
the large-scale model for such grouping. His <u>Ecclesiastical
Sketches</u> of 1832 seized upon the simple expedient of chronology
as a method of organization.

> Down a swift Stream, thus far, a bold design
> Have we pursued, with livelier stir of heart . . .
> We, nothing loth a lingering course to measure,
> May gather up our thoughts, and mark at leisure
> How widely spread the interests of our theme.

Here was a sort of holy river of time flowing past what Miss
Fenwick calls "the introduction, progress, and operation of the
Church of England". Like the river Duddon there were eddies
devoted to architecture and liturgy, but the main flow of events
moved forward in ordered pace: Part I "From the Introduction
of Christianity into Britain to the Consummation of the Papal
Domination" (39 sonnets), Part II "To the Close of Troubles in
the Reign of Charles I" (46 sonnets). It is significant that in
ordering the structure of this series Wordsworth emphasizes
beginning, middle, and end. In the often-quoted letter addressed
to the anthologist Dyce in 1833, he wrote:

> It should seem that the sonnet, like every other
> legitimate composition ought to have a beginning, a
> middle, and an end — in other words, to consist of
> three parts, like the three parts of a syllogism, if
> such an illustration may be used. But the frame of

metre adopted by the Italians does not accord with
this view; and, as adhered to by them, it seems to
be, if not arbitrary, best fitted to a division of the
sense into two parts, of eight and six lines each. (15)

This bipartite structure of the Italian sonnet, to which
Wordsworth adheres in the main, could thus be balanced against
the tripartite architectonics of the whole.

Milton had furnished the model for a religious sonnet of lofty
dignity; Wordsworth had lifted the subject matter above partisan
religion, muted its tone, and suggested methods of ordering
longer poems of sonnet groups. The poets of the nineteenth
century— a century much concerned with Christian faith —
followed the lead. Taking Wordsworth as an archetype, Isaac
Williams composed 204 sonnets entitled The Altar (1847), describing biblical events from Gethsemane to the Ascension.
Like the liturgy group in Ecclesiastical Sonnets, Sir Aubrey de
Vere's twenty-three sonnets On The Lord's Prayer echo the
petitions of church ritual. Hartley Coleridge wrote a loosely
organized group of thirty-three Sonnets on Scriptural and Religious Subjects. Mrs. Hemans, whom Wordsworth called a
"holy spirit", composed fifteen sonnets on Female Characters
of Scripture, and in 1840 Frederick Faber published The Four
Religious Heathen: Herodotus, Nicias, Socrates, and Seneca.
Tennyson Turner indicated his attitude toward the Oxford Movement in Christ and Orpheus. As the century moved on, the religious tradition weakened, but the minor poets continued.
Richard Wilton, imitating Wordsworth's chronological methods
of organization, composed Sonnets on the Fathers and Sonnets
on the Types; John Charles Earle composed religious sequences
whose parts numbered in the hundreds; and Edward Lefroy
described Windows of the Church as Wordsworth had pictured
architectural details of chapels and abbeys. In the last decade
of the century Christina Rossetti published several short sequences and a longer group of seventeen sonnets, Out of the
Deep Have I Called Unto Thee, which reflects in her almost
flawless sonnet technique the deep convictions of her Christian
faith.

Because Wordsworth naturally assumed the polity of church
and state in planning the Ecclesiastical Sketches, many of the
sonnets are political as well as religious in subject matter: "The
Norman Conquest", "Gunpowder Plot", "Elizabeth", "Charles II",

for example. But Wordsworth also wrote political and historical
sequences, which seem looser in structure than any of his other
sonnet series. When he first published Sonnets upon the Punishment of Death, they appeared in the Quarterly Review with an
expository prose commentary by Sir Henry Taylor, helping to
link these facets of prosaic ideas. Realizing the weakness of
his total concept, Wordsworth justified his structure in a letter
to Sir Henry: "Where I have a large amount of Sonnets in series,
I have not been unwilling to start sometimes with a logical connective of a 'Yet' or a 'But'. Here, however, as the series is
not long, I wished that each sonnet should stand independent of
such formal tie . . ."(16) One rather suspects that it is not the
length but the subject matter that makes expedient the almost
separateness of each sonnet. In a much shorter sequence,
written at about the same time and not concerned with a political
issue, Wordsworth begins the third sonnet with "But why that
prayer?" (17) His other long political sequence, Sonnets to
Liberty and Order (1845), was composed chiefly of sonnets
written and first published as separate poems or in shorter
groups. The title of one of these shorter groups bespeaks the
unmalleability of political history as subject matter for sonnet
sequences: In Allusion to the Various Recent Histories and
Notices of the French Revolution. Coleridge, who had worked
earlier in this same tradition, apparently never felt that Sonnets
on Eminent Characters (over half of whom were political figures)
had any real unity. After their serial newspaper publication, he
reprinted most of the sonnets only as separate poems. In 1839
Martin Tupper, that Victorian entrepreneur par excellence,
published A Modern Pyramid: to Commemorate a Septuagint of
Worthies with an accompanying moralizing prose discourse on
each of his seventy figures of legend and history: from Cain and
Abel to Lord Nelson. At the end of the Victorian age William
Michael Rossetti was continuing the tradition. In 1907 he published fifty Democratic Sonnets, dedicated to the memory of
Dante Gabriel. In the Prefatory Note he says:

> I began this series with the intention of treating any
> subjects, of a democratic or progressive kind, proper
> to the period of my own life, which commenced 1829.
> I contemplated writing 100 sonnets . . . When I dis-
> continued adding to the series, I set the whole affair
> aside, but now at last it sees the light.

The only unifying principle, then, is the "progressive" events of the writer's lifetime, filled out in the Elizabethan manner to half a _centurie_ of sonnets. In Miltonic fury William Michael lashes out against the Corn Laws of 1846 and England's policy of expedient encouragement to the Confederate States of America in 1861:

> . . . And now thou floutest at the man who frees
> The black and fettered limbs, while blessings rave,
> Rave mid thy jeers, for slavery's cause outworn.

Perhaps the best work in the political sequence of the Victorian period was done by Swinburne. His _Dirae_ contains twenty-four sonnets written from 1869-1873. The individual poems, though powerful in invective tone and metrical skill, have no further unifying principle than that of a gathering of "furies" against Ferdinand II of Naples, Pope Pius IX, the Austrian Empire, and Napolean III (on the day of whose death in 1873 Swinburne wrote "The Descent into Hell"). (18) In shorter sequences Swinburne fulminated against the House of Lords for honoring itself in elevating Tennyson to the peerage — _Vos Deos Laudamus_ — and against Gladstone in _Apostasy_. William Watson deplored the growing spirit of Imperialism in Britain with _Ver Tenebrosum: Sonnets of March and April 1885_, while Watts-Dunton gloried in _The Work of Cecil Rhodes_. The shadow and power of Milton's single sonnets thus dominated the political tradition of the sonnet sequence, and no Victorian poet improved the loose formula of unifying historical sonnets chiefly by tone and title first used by Cartwright, Coleridge, and Wordsworth.

The remaining categories of subject matter — literature and criticism, death and commemoration, personal life and philosophy — have fared little better than history and politics as unified sequences. Fewer poets have worked in these genres; the scope of the subject matter has remained somewhat miscellaneous and the structure somewhat loose. Just as Coleridge had commemorated eminent characters in 1794 and 1795, so in 1797 he parodied in three "mock sonnets" the "doleful egotism" and the "elaborate and swelling language" of his own poems and those of Charles Lloyd and Charles Lamb. In 1814 Capel Lofft in his five-volume sonnet anthology, _Laura_, included his own sequence of sonnets on the sonnet as his final blow against "those who affect to laugh at _Sonneteers_ and despise this whole Class of

Authors as unworthy of the Name of Poets". The title <u>La Corona</u>:
<u>The Wreath</u> he borrowed from John Donne, and his technique of
linking each sonnet to a line in the introductory sonnet was derived
also from Donne.

> The Worth of Verse is given to few to know;
> And on the Sonnet fewer still bestow
> That Wreath which Taste, Feeling and Judgement twine.

> Yet with those few peculiar is its Claim.
> I see its Glory rise; I see its Name
> Grace the celestial Lyre in Characters divine.

At the end of the century John Addington Symonds in better verse
was still writing about the sonnet. The tradition of commemorating poets and artists in series instead of single sonnets continued throughout the century. Leigh Hunt praised <u>The Author
of "Ion"</u>, Matthew Arnold the actress Rachel, and <u>Oscar Wilde</u>
recorded his <u>Impressions du Théâtre</u>. Just as he had fulminated
against Napoleon III in <u>Dirae</u>, Swinburne glorified <u>English
Dramatic Poets (1590-1650)</u> in twenty-one sonnets and condemned
the publication of Keats's love letters in <u>In Sepulcretis</u>.
   In the same vein as the sequences concerning literature and
criticism are those that have an elegiac cast. Although not a
prolific tradition, commemorative sonnets appeared throughout
the century. This tradition falls into two parts: those about death
in general and those commemorating the death of a particular
person. In 1781 Charles Emily had written after the manner of
the Graveyard poets, and in 1869 was published Clough's <u>Seven
Sonnets [on the Thought of Death]</u>. The personalized elegiac
sonnets, however, were more popular. Mrs. Browning wrote
three about her friend Hugh Stuart Boyd; Marston, six <u>Sonnets
to C.N.M.</u> (his sister); and after his death both Swinburne and
Watts-Dunton wrote elegiac sequences to the memory of
Marston. One of the longest Victorian elegiac sequences is
Lee-Hamilton's <u>Mimma Bella</u>. (19) Here in twenty-nine sonnets
a father recalls the memory of his little daughter Persius, whom
the Italian neighbors in Florence called "Mimma Bella". Although
there is almost no progression or resolution of thought, each
sonnet relates an incident or makes a comparison designed to
call to life the image of a baby now slipped "into the nursery
that men call death". The best poetry in point of diction, imagery

and lyric line is Swinburne's A Sequence of Sonnets on the
Death of Robert Browning, but like the other elegiac sequences
there is little method of unity for the poem as a whole.

The sequences about personal life and philosophy have little
claim to integrated wholes; many follow the manner of stream
of consciousness. Wordsworth in a group of four sonnets,
Personal Talk (1807), writes of the joys of silence, of childlike
perception, of books, and of poets who have made us heirs of
Truth. Near the end of the century John Addington Symonds in
a group of 140 sonnets (some in shorter sequences), called
Animi Figura (1884), meditates upon the patterns of his intellect: its memories and powers of growth—a sort of imitative
Wordsworthian Prelude. Yet in the Preface Symonds comments:
"This book cannot claim strict unity of subject. Connecting
links . . . are wanting. Yet the fact that they [sonnets and
shorter sequences] are the product of one mind and deal with
cognate problems, gives it a certain unity of tone. . . ."
Occasionally this sort of sequence, where the outlines of autobiography are simple and the scope of years not too great,
achieves, like certain of the love sequences, a sort of implied
narrative unity. Such is the case with George Eliot's Brother
and Sister (1874). In eleven sonnets she recalls incidents in her
own life when she was a child of about five before her brother
Isaac was sent to school at Coventry. There are accounts about
being startled by a gypsy and about catching a fish—both of
which appear with slightly altered details in The Mill on the
Floss.

James Thomson (B. V.) in To Joseph and Alice Barnes recalls those happy moments when as a school teacher in
Ballincollig, Ireland, he lived with the Barneses. There the
poet of "The City of Dreadful Night" tells of his love for his
"Good Angel" and her untimely death:

Indeed you set me in a happy place . . .
For there my own Good Angel took my hand
    And filled my soul with glory of her eyes,
And led me through the love-lit Faerie Land
    Which joins our common world to Paradise . . .
Ah, ever since her eyes withdrew their light,
I wander lost in blackest stormy night.

David Gray's thirty sonnets, In the Shadows (1862), likewise recall the tragedy of his search for fame, but because they sweep through the events and memories of his entire life — brief though it was — they presuppose a knowledge of the facts of that life for unifying the sequence.

Thus with these autobiographic series the discussion of subject matter and the methods of unifying individual sonnets comes full circle. In fact, the loosely autobiographic sequences like Christina Rossetti's Later Life and Philip Bourke Marston's Three Sonnets on Sorrow can be considered both amatory and personal philosophic poems. The two broad traditions, then, of some 250 nineteenth-century sonnet sequences are the amatory and the descriptive-meditative. Mrs. Browning and Rossetti established the archetypes of the amatory-lyric tradition with an emphasis on individual sonnets linked by an implied thread of "story" in Sonnets from the Portuguese and by theme and mood in The House of Life. Meredith's Modern Love, the archetype of the amatory-narrative tradition, placed the emphasis on the whole rather than on individual sonnets. The descriptive-meditative tradition is broad in subject matter and loose in overall structure. Wordsworth, whose sequences are chiefly products of Victorian times, composed the archetypal series in this tradition, and in his critical statements about sonnet grouping and in The River Duddon, Ecclesiastical Sketches, Poems Composed or Suggested during a Tour in the Summer of 1833, Sonnets upon the Punishment of Death, Personal Talk he recognized the problem of this genre and furnished models for its varied subject matter that were imitated throughout the century. Although the sonnets in these series may not be among Wordsworth's best poetry, they form an impressive accomplishment viewed in the light of their widespread influence on Victorian poets.

Finally, of significant interest is the fact that the term sonnet sequence itself is a Victorian innovation. When Hall Caine was preparing an anthology of sonnets that he later called Sonnets of Three Centuries, Rossetti wrote him several suggestions:

> I have thought of a title for your book. What think you of this?
>   A Sonnet Sequence
> from Elder to Modern Work, with Fifty
> Hitherto Unprinted Sonnets by Living
>   Writers.
> That would not be amiss. Tell me if you think of using

the title A Sonnet Sequence, as otherwise I might
use it in the House of Life. . . . What do you think
of this alternative title:
   The English Sonnet Muse
from Elizabeth's Reign to Victoria's. . . .
Treasury has been sadly run upon. (20)

Since Hall Caine did not use the title, Rossetti called his House
of Life a Sonnet-Sequence. From him the term was borrowed by
Swinburne in A Sequence of Sonnets on the Death of Robert
Browning (1890) and by William Sharp in Sonnet-Sequence (1894).
With John Addington Symonds and Blunt, two of the most prolific
writers of sonnet sequences among the Victorians, the term
passed into common usage. W. H. Auden calls a recent group of
twenty sonnets The Quest: A Sonnet Sequence, and Conrad Aiken
likewise uses the phrase "A Sonnet Sequence" as the subtitle for
And in the Human Heart. The term sequence has thus become
standard for present-day sonnet groupings; it has, in general,
replaced the Elizabethan centurie as well as series and cycle,
which were popular in the first part of the nineteenth century. (21)
   While suggesting the new term sequence Rossetti naturally uses
the word series as he continues discussing with Hall Caine the
aesthetic principles involved in grouping sonnets. But in 1794
Coleridge indicates in a letter to the editor of the Morning Chronicle that the term series is relatively new: "Mr. Editor — if, Sir,
the following Poems will not disgrace your poetical department,
I will transmit you a series of Sonnets (as it is the fashion to call
them) addressed like these to eminent contemporaries".
Wordsworth, the most important writer of groups of sonnets in
the first half of the nineteenth century, is always careful to label
his more closely unified cycles as series or sonnets in series.
Thus the two principal terms in the nineteenth century for poems
made up of sonnets were series, used by Coleridge and Wordsworth, and sequence, used by Dante Gabriel and Christina Rossetti,
Swinburne, Symonds, and Blunt.
   Critics and editors were quick to see the usefulness of the new
term sequence, and they applied it backwards to almost all previously written sonnet groups as a synonym for the outworn cycle
and series. Henry W. Meikle in 1914, when editing for the Scottish
Text Society the manuscript poetry of William Fowler, secretary
to Queen Ann (wife of James VI of Scotland) and uncle of Drummond
of Hawthornden, labeled an unentitled group of sixteen sonnets

"[A Sonnet Sequence]". But so acceptable has the term become to Renaissance scholars that frequently Fowler's sonnets masquerade under the Victorian label without brackets.

As a prosodic term the sonnet has been defined probably to its own detriment, especially by the prescriptive critics of the nineteenth century. It has been so "canonized" and "legislated" against that the most pertinent question to be asked in judging any sonnet is not whether the form is strictly Petrarchan or Shakespearean, but whether it is a poem. This was evidently the feeling of Tennyson, who once, according to Allingham, remarked "I never care to read a perfect sonnet. I look down the rhymes and that's enough. (22)

The sonnet sequence, however, has rarely been defined. As a prosodic term it has been considered either self-evident or something of a paradox. The nineteenth-century critics were too much concerned with the prosody of the individual sonnet to be aware of the widespread experimentation of the poets in linking sonnets into poems of unique unity. Jakob Schipper sees only that the sonnets of Sidney, Shakespeare, and Wordsworth occasionally exhibit a "strophic character". Mark Pattison praises Milton for freeing the sonnet of the shackling practice of writing poems in "fourteen line stanzas". And T. W. H. Crosland believes "the average sonnet sequence is really a sonnet surfeit". The twentieth-century writers of prosodic handbooks do little better; in fact, they succeed in saying no more about the sonnet sequence than the Oxford English Dictionary: "a set of sonnets connected in themes". Houston Peterson, however, in his anthology The Book of the Sonnet Sequence is aware of the history and the complexity of the genre. The patterns vary from a story told step by step in sonnet stanza (Blunt's Esther or Leonard's Two Lives), a poetic commentary on a story told indirectly or by implication (Shakespeare's sonnets or Meredith's Modern Love), a series of variations on a theme (Donne's Holy Sonnets, Rossetti's House of Life, or Rupert Brooke's 1914) or an emotionally colored description of some phase of nature or history (Wordsworth's River Duddon or Thomas S. Jones's Christ in Britain). It was the Victorian poets, then, who broadened the tradition of the sonnet sequence and added new complexity and significance to an old genre.

NOTES

(1) Les Sonnets élisabéthains (Paris: Libraire Ancienne Honoré Champion, 1929), p. 291.
(2) Elizabethan Sonnets (London: Constable, 1904), I, lxxxvii.
(3) Yet George Wither produced two long works composed of sonnet stanzas: Campo-Musae (1643) and Vox Pacifica (1645). Together these two poems contain almost 700 stanzas in the form of the Shakespearean sonnet. The stanzas are printed with no space between them, but with an indention after each couplet. Some of these "sonnets" are understandable poems; others, because of allusions and pronominal references, are not detachable. Despite much doggerel these works are interesting in that they anticipate similar experiments in the late nineteenth century by Swinburne and Blunt.
(4) Charles Bradford Mitchell, "The English Sonnet in the Seventeenth Century, especially after Milton", Summaries of Theses, 1938 (Harvard University, 1940), pp. 240-241.
(5) Raymond D. Havens, The Influence of Milton on English Poetry (Cambridge, Mass.: Harvard Univ. Press, 1922), p. 525. (Of these three thousand only about one hundred appeared between 1700 and 1775.)
(6) Paul Everett Reynolds, "The English Sonnet Sequence, 1783-1845", Summaries of Theses, 1938 (Harvard University, 1940), p. 329. Some Elizabethan poets, however, used a somewhat similar plan of grouping sonnets in series for dedicatory and commemorative purposes. Such, for example, were Gabriel Harvey's group of twenty-three Four Letters and Certain Sonnets touching Robert Greene (1592), the forty sonnets by Joshua Sylvester addressed to Henry IV of France "upon the late miraculous peace in France" (1599), and Constable's series of six to noble patronesses (ca. 1592).
(7) Since three of the sequences are written by Coleridge, Southey, Lamb and Lloyd who belong by virtue of their major publication to the nineteenth century, it can perhaps rightly be said that there are even fewer sequences written by eighteenth-century poets.
(8) According to the estimates of Miss Janet Scott and Sir Sidney Lee, Elizabethan poets produced over two thousand sonnets — singly and in series. The Victorians, in my Representative List of Sonnet Sequences in the Appendix, wrote over 4,000 sonnets,

and over three times that many not in sequence could readily be listed.

(9) It can reasonably be assumed that the traditions of the sonnet itself have been relatively well established. Although poets and critics from Gascoigne, James VI of Scotland, and John Hughes to Coleridge, Keats, Rossetti, and Watts-Dunton have all had their peculiar theories of what constitutes a good sonnet, the form has remained fixed in basic patterns.

(10) Paull F. Baum, ed., Rossetti's Poems, Ballads and Sonnets (New York: Doubleday, 1937), p. xxxvii.

(11) Albert Joseph Guérard, Robert Bridges: A Study of Traditionalism in Poetry (Cambridge, Mass.: Harvard Univ. Press, 1942), p. 76.

(12) Wordsworth is also the most prolific sonneteer among the major English poets: 532 sonnets (Raymond D. Havens, "Milton's Influence on Wordsworth's Early Sonnets", PMLA, LXIII [June, 1948], 752). Among the Elizabethans Henry Lok produced about 400; among nineteenth-century poets Sir Egerton Brydges left over 2000 in manuscript to the British Museum, Isaac Williams wrote about 374, Charles Tennyson Turner 342, Aubrey Thomas de Vere 324, Blunt 330, and Symonds 340. But none of these figures compares with the reputed production of the contemporary American poet, Merrill Moore: 50,000 in eighteen years.

(13) It should be noted that Wordsworth does not use the subtitle "Sonnets in Series" or "A Series of Sonnets" with these groups predominantly composed of sonnets nor with groups partly composed of sonnets like Memorials of a Tour on the Continent, 1820 (1822). The sub-titles he uses only in groups composed entirely of sonnets: Ecclesiastical Sonnets, The River Duddon, Sonnets upon the Punishment of Death.

(14) "The Influence of Milton and Wordsworth on the Early Victorian Sonnet", ELH, V (September 1938), 233. Since Mr. Sanderlin has examined over 6000 sonnets between 1800-1850, his opinion carries weight.

(15) The Letters of William and Dorothy Wordsworth: The Later Years, ed. E. de Selincourt (Oxford: Clarendon Press, 1939), II, 652-53.

(16) Letters, III, 1097.

(17) Here Wordsworth in criticism and practice puts his finger on a crucial question of the structure of sonnet sequences: Is the sonnet series a group of individual poems or a single poem in sonnet stanzas? In the Fenwick note to this short sequence The

Widow on Windermere Side (1842) the poet commented: "It is
scarcely worth while to notice that the stanzas are written in
sonnet form, which was adopted when I thought the matter might
be included in twenty-eight lines".
(18) It is not surprising that Swinburne, who used 420 metrical
forms to Tennyson's 240 (The Best of Swinburne, ed. Clyde K.
Hyder and Lewis Chase [New York: Nelson, 1937], p. xxviii),
should have taken the sonnet sequence to its metrical non plus
ultra. In Locrine he uses sonnet rhythm and rime scheme (but
not sonnet structure of thought) for Act I, sc. 2 and Act V, sc. 1.
(19) Eugene Lee-Hamilton (1845-1907) was a prolific writer of
sonnet sequences. In 100 Imaginary Sonnets (1888) he allows
historical and legendary figures to speak at moments of crisis
(reminiscent of Landor's Imaginary Conversations); in 103
Sonnets of the Wingless Hours (1894) he recounts his thoughts
during twenty years upon a "wheeled bed". (There is no adequate
biographical or critical study of Lee-Hamilton.)
(20) T. Hall Caine, Recollections of Dante Gabriel Rossetti
(London: Elliot Stock, 1882), p. 244.
(21) Actually the term sequence was first used in this sense by
George Gascoigne. Critic as well as poet and storyteller,
Gascoigne introduces a group of three sonnets in Poem 41 of
A Hundreth Sundrie Flowres (1572/3): "Three Sonnets in sequence
and written upon this occasion" (see my "Gascoigne and the Term
'Sonnet Sequence'", N&Q 1 N.S. [1954], 189-91; and "The Term
Sonnet Sequence", MLN 64 [1947], 400-02).
(22) William Allingham, A Diary, ed. H. Allingham and
D. Radford (London: Macmillan, 1907), p. 302.

2. THE TENNYSONS AND THE ROSSETTIS: SONNETEERING FAMILIES

(A)

One measure of the Victorian revival of interest in the sonnet is apparent from the family contributions of the Tennysons and the Rossettis. The very quantity of their production is surprising. Together the brothers Tennyson wrote some four hundred sonnets. Alfred is known to have written fifty-two. (1) The Collected Sonnets, Old and New (1880) of Charles, the most prolific sonneteer among the brothers, contains 342. Frederick, the oldest brother, did not publish his first volume Days and Hours until 1854 when he was forty-seven. It contains only two sonnets. In 1895 at the age of eighty-eight he published a fourth volume Poems of the Day and Year, which contains three sonnets. Of the four other brothers only Edward is known to have written poetry, and his only published lyric was a sonnet in the Yorkshire Literary Annual. (2)

Together the three Rossettis also wrote about four hundred sonnets, which are for the most part superior in poetic quality to those of the Tennysons. And if translations of sonnets are included, the total would be considerably higher since Dante Gabriel, who learned his sonnet craftsmanship in that process, translated some 175 in The Early Italian Poets (1861). Translations aside, William Michael included 190 sonnets in The Works (1911), and there are fifteen additional ones in Paull F. Baum's An Analytical List of Manuscripts in the Duke University Library, with Hitherto Unpublished Verse and Prose (1931). The case of Christina is more difficult to state with accuracy. Before she died Christina published seventy-six sonnets in Poems, New and Enlarged (1892), but William Michael both added and subtracted sonnets in his two posthumous editions of her poems, New Poems (1896) and Poetical Works (1904). Before a definitive number is established for either Christina's or Dante Gabriel's sonnets, there need to be accurate, scholarly editions of their works. As for William Michael himself, his only book-length poetical work is fifty Democratic Sonnets (1907), and in 1971 Victorian Studies printed an additional fourteen that William

Michael did not choose to include. Together, then, the Tennysons and the Rossettis produced about eight hundred sonnets exclusive of translations.

For both the Tennysons and the Rossettis the writing of poetry in the beginning was a family enterprise. The three Tennysons were separated in age by only one year (Frederick being born in 1807, Charles in 1808, and Alfred in 1809), and the isolation of tiny Somersby in Lincolnshire forced the boys onto their own resources for amusement. About 1820 Alfred's first attempt at poetry "was made at the instigation of his brother Charles. Little Alfred was kept indoors by a cold one Sunday when the rest of the family went to church, and Charles suggested that he should see if he could write poetry, giving as a subject the praise of flowers. When the party came back from church, Alfred had covered both sides of a large slate with blank verse lines in the style of Thomson, the only English poet known to him at the time". (3) Later Charles and Alfred often walked on opposite sides of a hedge composing poetry aloud and "shouting to each other any particularly fancied line as, for example, one of Alfred's that Charles long remembered: A thousand brazen chariots rolled over a bridge of brass". (4) The combination of Dr. Tennyson's well-stocked library and the Somersby countryside led Alfred to some remarkable early poems imitative of Milton, Beaumont and Fletcher, and Scott. Sharing an attic bedroom, the "darling room" of Alfred's 1832 poem:

Not any room so warm and bright
Wherein to read, wherein to write. — (5)

The three brothers made poetry a game, often communal, some-times private; and Poems by Two [Three] Brothers (1827), before their Cambridge days, was one result. It was not, however, until 1828 when the brothers met Arthur Hallam, who had been to Italy, learned Italian, and even written poems in Italian, that the sonnet became a part of their poetic repertoire.

In that year Alfred Tennyson and Arthur Hallam together wrote a sonnet "To Poesy", which begins, "Religion be thy sword; the armoury/ Of God shall yield it tempered. . . ." The joint author-ship is specified in the Heath MS, and Hallam noted on his copy: "I had some hand in the worst part of this". (6) Alfred also wrote at least two other irregular sonnets that same year: a second "To Poesy", which begins, "O God, make this age great that we

may be / As giants in Thy Praise", and "Among some Nations
Fate hath placed too far / The lamps of song have never risen
or set". And in the summer term of 1829 Arthur Hallam wrote
a sonnet to Alfred Tennyson beginning, "Oh, last in time, but
worthy to be first / Of friends in rank. . . ." These poems
mark Alfred's early association with the sonnet form as well as
the high-minded ideals of the Apostles, the Cambridge undergraduate society he and Hallam joined in the spring of 1829.
Indeed, in later life many of the Apostles continued their interest
in the sonnet. Richard Trench and Monkton Milnes composed
individual sonnets and sequences. And James Spedding edited
Charles Tennyson's Collected Sonnets after the author's death.
   As for the young Tennysons, both Charles and Alfred dis-
played their new interest in the sonnet in their separate volumes
of 1830. In Poems, Chiefly Lyrical Alfred printed a group of
sonnets and a sequence of three called "Love". Charles, whose
interest in the sonnet was more enthusiastic and more lasting
than his brother's, titled his volume Sonnets and Fugitive Pieces,
and his next volume in 1864 he called simply Sonnets.
   The development of the three young Rossettis' interest in the
sonnet was both similar to and different from that of the
Tennysons. The Rossettis were a London family, father
Gabriele being an Italian immigrant — "a man of letters, a
custodian of ancient bronzes in the Museo Borbonico of Naples,
and a poet" — in the words of his younger son William Michael. (7)
Mrs. Rossetti was Frances Polidori before her marriage, being
one-half Italian. The children were thus "three-fourths Italian".
With this background and predisposition it is not surprising that
sonnets interested them. Like the Tennysons the boys shared
sleeping quarters as well as a communal curiosity about poetry.

   In the later part of 1848 and in 1849 [when they were at
   the end of their teens, William Michael says] my brother
   practised his pen to no small extent in writing sonnets to
   bouts-rimés. He and I would sit together in our bare little
   room at the top of No. 50 Charlotte Street, I giving him
   the rhymes for a sonnet, and he me the rhymes for
   another; and we would write off our emulous exercises
   with considerable speed, he constantly the more rapid of
   the two. (8)

Occasionally, though not often, Christina joined in the bouts-

rimés: ". . . being in my company at Brighton in the summer
of 1848 [writes William Michael], she consented to try her
chance. Like her brothers, she was rapid at work. The first
sonnet in this present series [New Poems] was done in nine
minutes; the ninth in five".(9) Speed, though it attested a youthful facility, did not remain the goal of Dante Gabriel and
Christina; their major works in sonnet form — The House of Life
and Monna Innominata — were slow in evolving. William Michael,
however, seems never to have escaped completely this childish
pattern of game-and-speed.

(B)

Unlike the rather considerable amount of criticism that has
been written about the sonnets of Dante Gabriel and Christina
Rossetti, surprisingly little has been said about the sonnets of
Alfred Tennyson when one considers the quantity of commentary
on most of his poetry. Dougald B. MacEachen in "Tennyson and
the Sonnet" examines forty-six, establishing the fact that the
sonnets fall into two periods: those written when the poet was
between nineteen and twenty-nine and a small group of eight
written when he was past sixty — the sonnet "To W. C. Macready"
(1851) isolated in the mid-years. The early sonnets are more
personal and lyric, the later ones more occasional and per-
functory. Of the late sonnets three were intended as prefaces
to plays: "Guess well, and that is well" for Queen Mary, "Show-
Day at Battle Abbey" for Harold, and "Old ghosts whose day was
done ere mine began" for Becket. Five were occasioned by
literary events: James Knowles, editor of the new Nineteenth
Century, requested something from Tennyson, and "Prefatory
Sonnet to the 'Nineteenth Century'", "Montenegro", and "To
Victor Hugo" were the laureate's compliance. And "To the Rev.
W. H. Brookfield" was written for the posthumous edition of the
Sermons of Tennyson's friend of Cambridge days. Like Browning,
then, the sonnet finally became for the aging Tennyson a graceful way to discharge a literary chore: prefaces, memorials, and
requests for lyrics.

The forty-three early sonnets(10) are varied in subject matter,
tone, and metrics. Seventeen concern love — chiefly about Rosa
Baring and Sophy Rawnsley. In tone they vary from juvenile
sentimentalism to the religious poise of "The Christian Penitent".

In metrics they are irregular in the main, using twenty-seven rime patterns. Indeed some are sonnets almost solely by virtue of their fourteen lines.

Tennyson himself seemed strangely aware of the inadequacy of his sonnet structure. Of the seven sonnets in Poems, Chiefly Lyrical he reprinted only "To J. M. K." Of the seven sonnets in the 1832 volume J. F. A. Pyre finds that they "show considerable progress toward an observance of the conventional form [two-part structure]". (11) Yet even among these Tennyson excluded two from his collected works.

Even more strange is Tennyson's reaction to his better sonnets. Most critics agree that the second sonnet in Three Sonnets to a Coquette is among his best:

> The form, the form alone is eloquent!
> A nobler yearning never broke her rest
> Than but to dance and sing, be gaily drest,
> And win all eyes with all accomplishment:
> Yet in the whirling dances as we went,
> My fancy made me for a moment blest
> To find my heart so near the beautious breast
> That once had power to rob it of content.
> A moment came the tenderness of tears,
> The phantom of a wish that once could move,
> A ghost of passion that no smiles restore —
> For ah! the slight coquette, she cannot love,
> And if you kissed her feet a thousand years,
> She still would take the praise, and care no more.

Tennyson withheld publication of this poem, written around 1836, until 1865. Undoubtedly autobiographical (Rosa Baring and his quarrel with her after a ball — the atmosphere of the dance episode in Maud), the sonnet like its subject has form that is eloquent: the modulation of vowels, the expert use of repetition, and the control of the sonnet structure. If the subject matter is thin and the tone a bit sentimental, the essence of Romantic lyricism is as surely here as in the songs from The Princess.

Another equally memorable sonnet is

> She took the dappled partridge fleckt with blood,
>   And in her hand the drooping pheasant bare,
>   And by his feet she held the woolly hare,

And like a master-painting where she stood,
Lookt some new Goddess of an English wood.
  Nor could I find an imperfection there,
  Nor blame the wanton act that showed so fair —
To me whatever freak she plays is good.
<u>Hers</u> is the fairest Life that breathes with breath,
  And <u>their</u> still plumes and azure eyelids closed
    Made quiet Death so beautiful to see
That Death lent grace to Life and Life to Death,
  And in one image Life and Death reposed,
    To make my love an Immortality.

Written during Tennyson's undergraduate days and never
published during his life, this is a remarkable production in the
same way that the second <u>Coquette</u> sonnet is. Indeed, if there
were a few more sonnets like these two, the case could easily
be made that there is a Tennysonian sonnet of lyric enchantment.
    For a poet as skillful in metrics as Tennyson this relative
failure as a sonneteer is puzzling. He wrote more sonnets than
Arnold and more than Meredith if the seizains of <u>Modern Love</u>
are excluded; and like these two poets he starts by preferring
irregular patterns and ends by espousing regular Italian forms
for occasional and trivial subject matter. Yet he never achieved
a poem to compare with Arnold's "Shakespeare" or Meredith's
"Lucifer in Starlight". Allingham records that in 1880 when
Tennyson was discussing some of the slacknesses of his brother
Charles's sonnets, he said: "I thought the other day of writing a
sonnet beginning — I hate the perfect Sonnet! After going on for
four lines I should say

    And now there's 'down' and 'crown' and 'frown' and 'brown':
    I'll take the latter. Then there's 'cheer' and 'fear' —
    And several others, —

and so forth, would it be worth doing?"(12) This attitude is close
to Browning's though for a different reason: Browning objects in
"House" and elsewhere to the dominant subject matter of sonnets —
their association with what he would consider private affairs;
Tennyson seems to object to the constricting demand of the
metrics. Yet after 1880 he goes on revising early sonnets like
"The Christian Penitent" (1832), which becomes "Doubt and
Prayer" (1892). And the quietly amusing "Poets and Their

Bibliographies" (1885) shows the complete mastery of the
metrical form that was evident in a few of the very early sonnets.
Many commentators have tried to explain this puzzle. Pyre
says that the sonnet "baffled Tennyson to the end of his days". (13)
But "Poets and Their Bibliographies" and a very few of the early
sonnets like "The form, the form alone is eloquent" negate this
judgment. Paull F. Baum says that Tennyson "never adjusted his
talents to the special requirements of this form. It cannot be said
that he was unable to master them; it must be that after sundry
trials he lost interest". (14) Whatever this cryptic statement may
mean, it seems to imply that there was something in Tennyson's
approach to poetry that feared constriction and fixed verse forms.
At least such seems to be the main explanation for MacEachen,
who says that Tennyson believed "that continual recourse to the
sonnet to give form to whatever could be handled within narrow
limits would discourage originality and invite the growth of
mechanical habits of composition such as Wordsworth fell into
in his later years". (15) These explanations are at best conjec-
tural, but when MacEachen states as his final point that the death
of Hallam "weakened the attraction of the sonnet for Tennyson",
one wonders if an opposite conjecture is not equally valid. Since
Hallam was his mentor in the sonnet, Tennyson intuitively felt
that he should not challenge comparison with his beloved dead
friend. He would not use the sonnet for his major ideas — he
would not write his "Elegies" for Hallam in a sonnet sequence.
So far as the sonnet was concerned Tennyson like Browning was
caught in a web of circumstances where good taste rather de-
manded foregoing that verse form. Then there was Charles, a
best-loved brother, who after 1830 made the sonnet his special
province.

(C)

When Charles Tennyson published his Sonnets and Fugitive Piece
in 1830, it was read and reviewed along with his brother Alfred's
Poems, Chiefly Lyrical, which appeared in the same year. For
some readers — Leigh Hunt and Coleridge among others — Charles
volume seemed the more promising. It may have been Charles's
fondness for the sonnet that partly earned him accolades from the
older Romantic sonneteers, for here was a young writer with a
sharp eye for details and a perpetuator of a tradition they had

sought to reestablish: ". . . indeed a large portion of these sonnets . . . stands between Wordsworth and Southey's, and partakes of the excellences of both".(16) And Leigh Hunt stated in his review (and said frequently to the circle of his listeners) that Charles's sonnets were superior to everything written since Keats's last volume.

After graduating from Cambridge in 1832, Charles Tennyson was placed on opium by a doctor's orders to relieve a "nervous complaint".(17) Recovering somewhat by 1836, he married Louisa Sellwood, the elder sister of Alfred's future wife Emily, and assumed the duties of the vicar of Grasby. Succeeding to his great uncle's property and adopting his name of Turner, Charles again succumbed to opium. His home was broken up, and the collapse of his marriage helped cause the constrained relationship in Alfred's engagement to Emily Sellwood. In 1849, however, Charles was reunited with Louisa, and until the end of their days they wrought good works among the simple people of their parish — a devoted, childless couple. As his routine became placid, Charles gradually returned to writing poetry though a second volume did not appear until 1864. Overshadowed by the prolific and varied muse of Alfred, Charles seemed more and more content with small observations and the limited music of the sonnet. In fact, one wonders whether he did not come to regard sonnet writing as a kind of therapy. When Canon Rawnsley visited the Tennyson Turners in January of 1876, he described Charles as looking like John Milton "as he sat and boomed out sonorously his favorite sonnets". As to his method of composing the poet said, "'I always like to write my sonnet in the morning, but I never judge of it till after dinner. If it runs and sounds well after dinner, I pass it'."(18)

In this manner Charles "passed" 342 sonnets about the incidents of his day that he wished to recollect in Wordsworthian tranquillity. "The Gold-Crested Wren: His relation to the Sonnet" is an example:

When my hand closed upon thee, worn and spent
With idly dashing on the window-pane,
Or clinging to the cornice — I, that meant
At once to free thee, could not but detain;
I dropt my pen, I left the unfinish'd lay,
To give thee back to freedom; but I took —
Oh, charm of sweet occasion! — one brief look

> At thy bright eyes and innocent dismay;
> Then forth I sent thee on thy homeward quest,
> My lesson learnt — thy beauty got by heart:
> And if, at times, my sonnet-muse would rest
> Short of her topmost skill, her little best,
> The memory of thy delicate gold crest
> Shall plead for one last touch, — the crown of Art.

Aware of the sonnet's limited scope as well as Alfred's broadening poetic interest, Charles invariably chooses the small matters of his personal world as subjects of implied larger concern: "The Mute Lovers on the Railway Journey", "Little Sophy by the Seaside", "Letty's Globe", "Julius Caesar and the Honey-Bee". Occasionally Charles's tone is bantering with good humor like "Calvus to a Fly", in which the insect mistakes the poet's bald pate for some new world of light.

Often, however, the serious tone points quietly toward the ominous implication. The pair of sonnets "The Steam Threshing-Machine" is illustrative:

> Flush with the pond the lurid furnace burned
> At eve, while smoke and vapor filled the yard;
> The gloomy winter sky was dimly starred,
> The fly-wheel with a mellow murmur turned. . . .
>
> The sweating statue, and her sacred wain
> Low-booming with the prophecy of steam.

Of this sonnet Alfred remarked to Canon Rawnsley's father in 1868: " 'It is no use my trying to write sonnets, when Charles can turn such music as that, upon an unmusical subject. . . . There is no one in the world that could write that sonnet but Charles'. "

Not only to the Rawnsleys did Alfred praise his brother's sonnets. William Allingham records in his Diary several similar comments: in 1867 "A. T., Charles T., and I go up High Street and out into a field beyond, where we sit on a balk of wood, looking at some cows grazing, and A. T. smoking. He quotes a sonnet of his brother's about elms and calls it daimonisch. " The next year when Alfred is writing his "San Grail", Allingham recalls another outing when they talk "on his brother Charles's Sonnets. 'All is not chemistry and matter'. "

And after Charles's death Alfred gave to Allingham's wife
Helen a copy of the collected edition "of his brother Charles's
Sonnets, about to be published, and one day read several of
them to her with feeling and warm praise. . . . 'I know the
place, the road, everything'."(19)

The comments of Alfred indicate clearly at least two things:
he thought of the sonnet as Charles's forte, and it should be
judged by the music, not the "matter". Knowing many of Charles's
sonnets by heart and resenting the constriction of that metrical
form, Alfred Tennyson seemed willing to leave the sonnet to
Arthur Hallam and Charles, his two favorite people. " 'I rank
my brother's sonnets next to those of the three Olympians —
Shakespeare, Milton, and Wordsworth'."(20) If this praise
seems excessively high, such an opinion was shared by Leigh
Hunt, Sir Henry Taylor, and even Wordsworth himself. But
Coleridge was more to the mark when despite his first enthusi-
asm he put his finger directly on Charles's fatal flaw: excessive
sentimentalism. Of the sonnet "On Startling Some Pigeons",
which ended:

> . . . While proud and sorrowing man,
> An eagle, weary of his mighty wings,
> With anxious inquest fills his little span.

Coleridge wrote: "A sweet sonnet, and with the exception of the
word 'little', faultless. 'Little' may be a proper word, if man
had been contemplated positively. He is not so comparatively
in his Eagle-relation to the pigeons."(21) And Coleridge sensed
the general weakness of Charles's sonnets when he wrote: "The
feeling seems to me fluttering and unsteady, pouncing and
skimming on a succession of truisms". (22)

Nevertheless, many of Charles Tennyson's contemporaries
found pleasant metrics, keen observation, and delicate sensi-
bilities in his sonnets. Spedding, in editing the collected edition,
divided the 342 poems into these groups: The Parson Poet; Men,
Women and Children; Earth, Sea and Sky; and Birds, Beasts and
Insects. Read in this arrangement the sonnets take on a loose
sequential quality. Some twenty-three of the first group, for
example, concern the Higher Criticism though Charles himself
extended no grouping beyond two or three. To a friend who
would "annotate Christ Jesus" with "flying leaves of legends
strange" Charles warns

50

Let Calvary stand clear of fabulous mist
Keep all the paths of Olivet for Christ
And let no Orphic phantom walk with Him!

Placed in a group these sonnets are quite representative of
contemporary attitudes towards current theology.

Charles Tennyson was at his best, however, when he was
writing about "Our New Church" and "Our New Church Clock"
rather than the arguments about the Higher Criticism. And he
is equally appealing when he chooses intimate subjects like
"The School-boy's Dream on the Night before the Holidays",
"The Lattice at Sunrise", and "The Old Fox-Hunter". His style
is always simple and clear, and he never hesitates to bend the
strict Italian sonnet pattern to his immediate need — an extra
foot in the last line or a division of thought where momentary
logic puts it. As a simple man Charles felt that he should make
the sonnet appear a natural "little" verse:

For I am bound by duties and constraints
To mine own land, or move in modest round
Among my neighbors. . . .
My love of home no circumstance can shake;
I and yon sycamore have grown together,
How on yon slope the shifting sunsets lie
None know like me and mine; and, tending hither,
Flows the strong current of my memory.

In 342 sonnets Charles Tennyson recorded his autobiography:
the sights, sounds, and thoughts of a poet-parson.

Of the three poetic Tennysons Frederick wrote the fewest
sonnets. Though he published three volumes of poetry after the
age of eighty-three, — he was a late bloomer — and that first
flowering occurred in Italy under the influence of Browning, who
was no lover of the sonnet. Frederick, unlike Charles, wrote in
windy generalities and with violent passion. The following sonnet from his Poems of the Day and Year (1895) is typical:

TO POESY

Tis not for golden eloquence I pray,
   A God-like tongue to move a stony heart:
   Full fain am I to dwell with thee apart

In solitary uplands far away,
And, thro' the blossoms of a bloomy spray,
  To gaze upon the wonderful, sweet face
  Of Nature in a wild and pathless place:
And if it were that I should once array,
In words of magic woven curiously,
  All the deep gladness of a summer morn,
Or rays of evening that light up the lea
  On dewy days of spring, or shadows borne
Athwart the forehead of an autumn noon —
Then would I die and ask no better boon!(23)

"To Poesy" was the title used by Alfred in one of his first
sonnets, and it was also the title of another he and Hallam
composed jointly. Having outlived both his brothers, Frederick
returned to the subject matter of Alfred and Arthur Hallam,
and like Charles used nature as his controlling image. But
there the similarities stop. The brothers Tennyson together —
Alfred too few and Charles too many — composed their four
hundred sonnets over a sixty year period, and, after the
Rossettis, were the most interesting sonneteering family of
the Victorian age.

(D)

The poetic reputations of the three Rossettis depend to a large
extent upon their sonnets. Dante Gabriel's The House of Life is
surely one of the major contributions to sonnet literature in the
English language. Christina's Monna Innominata: A Sonnet of
Sonnets and Later Life: A Double Sonnet of Sonnets, as well as
individual sonnets like "Remembrance", represent her distinc-
tive voice of quiet renunciation. And William Michael, known
chiefly as critic, editor, and family biographer, published only
one poetic work, Democratic Sonnets (1907) long after the deaths
of his brother and sister.
  The circumstances surrounding that work were, however, very
much a family affair; and like most things in the Rossetti family
intimately related to Dante Gabriel. William Michael, who had
written verse only infrequently since the exciting days of the
Pre-Raphaelite Brotherhood with its short-lived little magazine
The Germ, was urged early in 1881 to try his hand once again

at poetry. Dante Gabriel suggested, according to William, "a
series of 'Democratic Sonnets', dealing with appropriate events
of my own life-time". (24) William Michael apparently had
doubts about his poetic ability, for he says, "I . . . expressed
a certain reluctance (which had always been potent with me) to
come forward as a moderately good poet when I had a brother
and sister who were positively good poets, and recognized as
such". (25) Nevertheless, William started out with the energetic
devotion he usually manifested for his literary tasks: "I wrote
the first, on Garibaldi, when I was absent from London, in
January 1881, to deliver some lectures. I then for a while pro-
ceeded rapidly, scarcely a day passing when I did not draft a
sonnet — occasionally more than one."(26) Dante Gabriel found
these sonnets "not so fine as the very fine one on Garibaldi";
"I think he is doing them rather too fast", he wrote William's
wife Lucy. And to Frederic Shields, Gabriel confessed that
William's recent illness with a sore throat would doubtless
result in "two sonnets a day and inexorable politics". (27)

Dante Gabriel, who was trying desperately to finish his
volume Ballads and Poems in the midst of his failing health,
was perhaps not a good critic of his brother's work. Surprisingly he objects not so much to William's style which he found
"rather too Browningesque", but rather to the cast of the
material that he labeled " 'Tyrannicide', 'Fenianism', and other
incendiary subjects". (28) From one who had himself originally
suggested the political arena to William and who had himself
written sonnets under the influence of Swinburne with titles like
"At the Sunrise in 1848", "On the Refusal of Aid between Nations
and "Place de la Bastille, Paris", his attitude seems ironical,
to say the least. But distance always lends enchantment: Dante
Gabriel's political sonnets concerned foreign countries, not
England; William's, though treating subjects already explored
by Shelley, Wordsworth, Mrs. Browning, and even Ebenezer
Elliott, were about home as well as about foreign lands. But
what was more, William was a civil servant of the Inland
Revenue, the principal breadwinner for all the Rossettis, as he
had always been.

As he usually did, William bowed to Gabriel's opinion and put
his sonnets aside, citing pressure of other work and lack of a
publisher as his reasons. To Gabriel, however, he made it
clear that he saw through the pretenses: "I don't think that the
other persons who agree in your anxieties on the subject can

count for much. I suppose Watts [Swinburne's "keeper"] is the
principal person, & he can have read very little of the sonnets.
Perhaps Mamma & Christina also: but Mamma's great age &
Christina's isolated devoteeism diminish the practical importance
of their view."(29)

On February 11, 1881, William indicated in the privacy of
his diaries that he "Looked through the list (which I drew up a
few days ago) of 100 subjects, and brought it to approximately
true sequence".(30) By sequence he means chronology — not
what Dante Gabriel finally came to mean by his term sonnet-
sequence. The first sonnet was to be called "The Past", the
second "Napolean Returned (1841)"; the ninety-ninth, "Irish
Land (1881)", and the one hundredth, "The Future". But this
concept of organization he did not carry out. When he left off
writing the sonnets, he had completed seventy-two. Of these in
1906 he found only fifty-seven to be "good" and fifteen "bad".
Fifty of the good ones were published in 1907 in two paper-bound
volumes by Alston Rivers, Ltd. In his diaries William calls the
edition "a cheap series". He had given up the idea of historical
sequence, beginning with "The Past" and ending with "The
Future", and had settled for a geographical arrangement:
volume I contains "Great Britain and Ireland" (14), "France"
(10); volume II contains "Italy" (12), "Germany" (2), "Austria
and Hungary" (3), "Russia" (3), "America" (4), and "General"(1).
In the main, the sonnets describe events or people: "Irish Famine
and Emigration, 1846-60", "Wordsworth, 1850", "The Slaves
Freed", "Lincoln, 1865". The sonnets are workmanlike but
pedestrian. "Elizabeth Barrett Browning, 1861" is typical:

A silence falls upon the hearts of men,
And women's eyes thrill passionate with tears.
In Casa Guidi, Barrett Browning's years
Have ceased to flow; and Love their denizen,
And High Intent and Genius, twinned again,
And Poesy who murmured in her ears
The secrets memorized by bards and seers,
And Fame who minted on those years his reign,
Quit the cold breast till now their tabernacle.
And mid the men's and women's griefs a cry,
A cry of children, wails acutest throbs.
Proudly her England weeps; her Italy
O'er soul-wrung stately features draws a veil;
And very Womanhood, in blessing, sobs.

54

Perhaps the first sonnet, the "Dedication: To the Memory of
Dante Gabriel Rossetti" is among the most harmonious; the
sestet reads:

> Gabriel, accept what verse may dedicate —
> A brother's heart deep-dinted with the pang
> Of one remembered mortal Easter-day.
> Silent the lips which might have answered yes —
> Lips out of which the laden spirit rang
> Reverberant echoes — Love and Change and Fate.

Just as Dante Gabriel sent the introductory sonnet on the sonnet
in The House of Life to his mother as a birthday gift in 1880,
William Michael dedicated his series to its begettor and its
terminator. And in so doing, he raises the question in the last
line of whether the original title of Part I of The House of Life
may not have been "Love and Change" instead of "Youth and
Change", which Gabriel evidently preferred when he decided to
foster the impression that most of the sonnets were inspired by
Lizzie Siddal instead of Janey Morris. Oswald Doughty has
noted William's frequent misquotation of the word Love for Youth
in his prose comments about his brother's sequence, but the real
clincher is in the last line of this apposite and unrevised dedicatory sonnet, written soon after Gabriel's death. (31) Did
William's memory merely slip, or did he consciously or unconsciously even the score with Gabriel for bringing pressure
from family and friends to circumvent publication of Democratic
Sonnets until it was really too late for them to seem congent? At
the very least, William plants the careful, artistic hint that
Gabriel's poetic anatomy of Love was not to be trusted as chronology. The sibling rivalry of youthful bouts-rimés extends
beyond the grave.

(E)

The circumstances of composition as well as the nature of Dante
Gabriel's The House of Life and Christina's Monna Innominata
and Later Life are far more familiar than William Michael's
Democratic Sonnets. And justly so. The inwrought subtlety of

Gabriel's sonnets and the shining simplicity of Christina's have
compelled the attention of readers, critics and scholars. What
is significant, however, for the Rossettis as a sonneteering
family is that during the decade of the 1870's until 1881 all
three were writing long groups of sonnets. Dante Gabriel's
early ones had been seen in manuscript by many of his friends,
including Meredith, who had admired them at the time he was
composing his far different sonnets in Modern Love. Some had
been buried with Elizabeth Siddal and subsequently exhumed; a
few appeared in The Fortnightly Review in 1869, more were
privately printed that same year, and fifty were published in
Poems of 1870. There is little doubt that the sequence is essentially the work of the years 1869-71(32) though the earliest
sonnet dates from 1847 and the latest 1881, when the 102 sonnets appeared, "Nuptial Sleep" having been canceled.

   During these years Christina — having read Sonnets from the
Portuguese by "the Great Poetess of our own day and nation",
and aware of Dante Gabriel's struggles with the House of his
own life — composed sometime before 1882, according to
William Michael, her Monna Innominata: A Sonnet of Sonnets,
the Renaissance title being "a blind interposed to draw off
attention from the writer in her proper person". (33) Indeed
there is scarcely a single historical reference or image of any
sort except for the parallel to the Esther story in the eighth
sonnet — a device used to mark the volta of the sequence, from
restrained impetuosity to Christian resignation. The last six
sonnets are songs of renunciation: in the heavenly life all is
love; here on earth is but "Silence of love that cannot sing again".
If the epigraphs from Dante and Petrarch were to be omitted,
the sequence retitled "Part I. Youth and Change", and the more
miscellaneous twenty-eight sonnets of Later Life added as
"Part II. Change and Fate", the result would be Christina's
"House of Life". Granted the differences in sonnet style —
Gabriel's baroque, sustained imagery and Christina's simple,
muted blending of octave and sestet — the sequences published
by brother and sister in 1881 are remarkably similar in structure and idea. An account of the joys of life and love gives way
to renunciation or a hopeless hope. As Browning maintains, the
sonnet is, despite disguises and generalizations, an instrument
intensely associated with the personal confession. And like
Robert Bridges both Rossettis were detailing their personal
concepts of "The Growth of Love".

As a sonnet-writing family, the ambience of sonnet bouts-rimés of childhood remained with all three Rossettis. William Michael is "assigned" the task of recalling his "democratic" sympathies and is scolded for doing the job too fast, Gabriel agonizes over "Soul's Beauty" and "Body's Beauty" in private and in public in order to create his masterpiece, Christina observes this Pre-Raphaelite catharsis in the making and quietly and secretly becomes her own donna innominata.

The Tennysons and the Rossettis, despite the families' interest in sonnets, never knew each other. Chance and circumstance and backgrounds were against such happenings. Even the most famous member of each family seemed little aware of the other's sonnets Alfred published very few within Gabriel's lifetime, and the latter was probably unacquainted with Charles's sonnets, which would have had little appeal for a London artist of Gabriel's cast of mind. In 1850 the young Dante Gabriel sent his translation of the Vita Nuova to the new poet laureate who acknowledged it as "very strong and earnest". (34) It does seem strange, however, that after Rossetti's death when his young biographer William Sharp wrote to Tennyson, asking apparently about the famous meeting in 1855 (when Tennyson was reading from Maud, Browning was home from Italy, and Rossetti was sketching the poets) that the laureate should express no recollection:

"I have neither drawing nor painting by Rossetti . . . .
nor (as far as I know) have I the slightest recollection
of his being present when I was 'reading the proof sheets
of Maud'.".
"My acquaintance with him was in fact but acquaintance,
not an 'intimacy', though I would willingly have known
something more of so accomplished an artist". (35)

For Alfred Tennyson, then, Gabriel Rossetti, the greatest Victorian sonneteer, was only a painter — one of those Pre-Raphaelite fellows whom a reformed Millais had persuaded to help illustrate Moxon's new edition on his 1842 Poems and a sonneteer whose "Nuptial Sleep", Buchanan reported, Tennyson privately called the "filthiest thing he had ever read". (36)

If the Tennysons and the Rossettis were almost unaware of each other as sonneteering families, they were much aware of the interests and directions of the sonneteering among the members of their own family. In this respect they were somewhat

unlike the Coleridges and the de Veres in the first part of the
century. There the relationship was that of father and children —
it was largely that of emulation, continuation, and editing. With
the Victorian Tennysons and Rossettis the relationship was that
of the same generation — it was largely that of rivalry, renunciation, and imitation with a difference. To this extent it was
indeed a more subtle relationship. Charles and Alfred Tennyson
were early rivals in sonneteering, but with the death of Arthur
Hallam and the illnesses of Charles, Alfred consciously or unconsciously all but renounced that field to his brother. Among
the Rossettis the rivalry was life long because the sonnet was
a form that interested all three all their lives. As Dante Gabriel,
Christina, and William Michael developed their distinct sonnet
styles, the rivalry ceased to be obvious and became complementary. Christina's and Dante Gabriel's sequences are mirrored
reflections of their emotional natures and their views of life, and
William Michael had his way with his own sonnets after their
deaths.

More obvious, though, is the variety of subject matter that the
sonnets of the two families encompasses. If one of the chief
contributions of nineteenth-century sonneteers was the broadening
of the possible uses of the genre, the Tennysons and the Rossettis
are excellent microcosms of that tendency. Charles Tennyson,
following the lead of Wordsworth, recalled his own thoughts of
the day - the bees in his yard, little girls he saw on his walks,
and the sounds of neighboring church bells. The metrics and rimes
of his sonnets he bent to suit the occasion or his own mood.
Alfred began to feel his way toward a modernizing of the outworn
Elizabethan cult of the adoration of the heartless feminine beauty:
the English huntress who takes "the dappled partridge fleckt with
blood", whose "form, the form alone is eloquent". And Frederick
shouted in Shelleyan echoes of "dewy days of spring, or shadows
borne / Athwart the forehead of an autumn noon". The Rossettis
restored the sonnet to its stricter Italian forms and returned its
subject matter to endless contemporary and timeless changes on
fleshly and spiritual loves. For Dante Gabriel there were silent
noons, lingering kisses, nuptial sleep, and hopeless hopes. For
Christina there were remembrances of the first day of love,
renunciations because of love of Him, and enduring human love
as "strong as death". For the less inspired William Michael
there were the democratic heroes — literary, political, and
moral — who in extended Miltonic manner kept England and him-

58

self above "slavery's cause outworn". All of this and more the Tennysons and the Rossettis lyrically expounded in some eight hundred sonnets.

NOTES

(1) Dougald B. MacEachen ("Tennyson and the Sonnet", VN, No. 14 [1958] , pp. 1-8) states "forty-six", but unfortunately he does not list the titles; Christopher Ricks (The Poems of Tennyson [London: Longmans, 1969]) prints fifty-three, but carefully annotates the fact that "The Christian Penitent" is an early version of "Doubt and Prayer". Apparently the discrepancy lies in sonnets like "Why to Blush is Better than to Paint" (from the unpublished Harvard Notebook, which was perhaps unavailable to MacEachen; and it is not clear whether MacEachen counts "To Poesy [Religion be thy sword] " that was a joint composition with Arthur Hallam though MacEachen does mention it in the "detached" first footnote. Furthermore, it does not seem that MacEachen includes "Among some Nations Fate hath placed too far" (from the Heath MS), the two sonnets "To Rosa" and "To Sophy" (from H.D. Rawnsley, Memories of Tennyson [Glasgow: MacLehose, 1900]).
(2) Harold Nicolson, Tennyson's Two Brothers (Cambridge: Univ. Press, 1947), p. 7.
(3) Charles Tennyson, Alfred Tennyson (New York: Macmillan, 1949), p. 25.
(4) Charles Tennyson, p. 35.
(5) All texts of Alfred Tennyson are from The Poems of Tennyson, ed. Christopher Ricks (London: Longmans, 1969), (p. 460).
(6) Ricks, p. 169.
(7) The Works of Dante Gabriel Rossetti, ed. William M. Rossetti (London: Ellis, 1911), p. vii.
(8) The Works of Dante Gabriel Rossetti, p. xviii.
(9) Christina Rossetti, New Poems, ed. William Michael Rossetti (London: Macmillan, 1896), Notes, p. 378. R.W. Crump, who plans to edit Christina's complete poems, has published nine additional bouts-rimés sonnets in "Eighteen Moments' Monuments: Christina Rossetti's Bouts-Rimés sonnets in the Troxell collection", The Princeton University Library Chronicle, 33 (1972), 210-229.

(10) This group includes the five or six additional sonnets (listed in Ricks's edition) that were apparently not considered by MacEachen; for their titles see Note 1.

(11) Formation of Tennyson's Style (Madison, Wisc.: Univ. of Wisconsin Studies in Language and Literature, 1921), p. 38.

(12) William Allingham's Diary, ed. H. Allingham and D. Radford (London: Macmillan, 1907), p. 302.

(13) Pyre, p. 38.

(14) Tennyson Sixty Years After (Chapel Hill: Univ. of North Carolina Press. 1948), p. 73.

(15) MacEachen, p. 6.

(16) From Coleridge's notes written in the margins of his copy (now in the British Museum), quoted in A Hundred Sonnets of Charles Tennyson Turner, ed. John Betjeman and Sir Charles Tennyson (London: Rupert Hart-Davis, 1960), p. 128. (Quotations from Charles Tennyson Turner's sonnets are from this edition.)

(17) A Hundred Sonnets of Charles Tennyson Turner, p. 9.

(18) Rawnsley, p. 231.

(19) Allingham's Diary, pp. 154, 187, 302.

(20) Quoted in Nicolson, p. 30.

(21) Quoted from Coleridge's copy margins in A Hundred Sonnets, p. 128.

(22) Quoted by Nicolson, p. 30.

(23) The text is from Poems of the Day and Year (London: John Lane, 1895).

(24) Dante Gabriel Rossetti: His Family-Letters with a Memoir, ed. William Michael Rossetti (London: Ellis, 1895), II, 369.

(25) Some Reminiscences (New York: Scribner's, 1906), II, 474.

(26) Some Reminiscences, II, 474.

(27) Letters of Dante Gabriel Rossetti, ed. Oswald Doughty and J. R. Wahl (Oxford: Clarendon, 1965-67), pp. 2410, 2425.

(28) Letters of Dante Gabriel Rossetti, p. 2451.

(29) From an unpublished letter in the Angeli Papers at the University of British Columbia, cited in Leonid M. Arishtein and William E. Fredeman, "William Michael Rossetti's 'Democratic Sonnets' ", VS 14 (1971), 249. This excellently detailed essay, to which I am indebted, cites much more of the background of these sonnets than I have mentioned here.

(30) Arishtein and Fredeman, p. 243.

(31) A Victorian Romantic: Dante Gabriel Rossetti (London: Muller, 1949), p. 381; see also my "The Brothers Rossetti and

Youth and Love", PLL, 4 (1968), 334-335.
(32) Paull F. Baum, ed., Rossetti's Poems, Ballads and Sonnets
(New York: Doubleday, 1937), p. xxxvii.
(33) Poetical Works (with Memoir and Notes by William Michael
Rossetti) (London: Macmillan, 1904), p. 462.
(34) G.H. Fleming, Rossetti and the Pre-Raphaelite Brotherhood
(London: Rupert Hart-Davis, 1967), p. 147.
(35) William Sharp (Fiona Macleod): A Memoir compiled by his
wife, Elizabeth A. Sharp (New York: Duffield, 1910), p. 66.
(36) G.H. Fleming, That Ne'er Shall Meet Again: Rossetti,
Millais, Hunt, (London: Michael Joseph, 1971), p. 362.

3. BROWNING AND THE SONNET

Of the major Victorian poets Browning wrote the fewest sonnets. Tennyson, who composed no memorable sonnet, is known to have written fifty-two, thirty of which were published during his lifetime. (1) Though Arnold wrote only twenty-nine, this number represents almost one-fourth of his poetic titles. In fact, the Victorian age itself, influenced by the quality of Keats's sixty-odd sonnets and the quantity of Wordsworth's more than five hundred, was the most prolific time of the sonnet. (2) And the poetic reputations of Elizabeth Barrett Browning, Meredith, the Rossettis, Wilfrid Scawen Blunt, John Addington Symonds, Hopkins, and Bridges rest to a large degree on their sonnet sequences.

More significant than the paucity of Browning's sonnets is his attitude toward this verse form as expressed both directly and indirectly, by the poet himself and by the men and women he wrote about. Prejudiced about sonnet writing, Browning during most of his poetic career seems to denigrate this form of poetry because he associated it with an invasion of privacy even though he was "The Onlie Begetter" of the most popular sonnet sequence of the age — those sonnets he preferred disguised by the title "Sonnets from the Portuguese". For him the form seemed a bête noire that would not entirely vanish until he finally tamed it into that little something he occasionally had to write "to order" for the ever-popular albums, public and private.

Browning is known to have written only eleven sonnets, one of which was a translation from the Italian poet, G.B.F. Zappi (1667-1719). (3) Only three of these, which form a sequence, appeared in any collection of his poems published during his lifetime: "Moses the Meek" Browning used in a comic footnote on exaggeration to "Jochanan Hakkadosh". He directed his printer, "Print these sonnets in smaller type, after the Note". (4) All the other sonnets appeared only in magazines, newspapers, or anthologies; and they were never collected by the poet himself. The occasions for writing these sonnets, their dates, and publications have been carefully noted from Arthur Symons' An Introduction to the Study of Browning (1886) and The Browning

Society's Papers, to Sir Frederic Kenyon's ten-volume Centenary
Edition (1912) and New Poems (1914), to William C. DeVane's
A Browning Handbook (1955). For the purposes of this essay,
however, a list indicating the date of composition, the first
publication (in brackets), and the subject matter of each will be
helpful:

1. "Eyes Calm Beside Thee", 1834 [Monthly Repository, 1834],
   adoration from a speechless lover.
2. The "Moses" of Michael Angelo, translated 1850 [Cornhill,
   1914], praise of a great work of a great sculptor.
3. Helen's Tower, 1870 [Pall Mall Gazette, 1883], admiration
   for Helen, Lady Dufferin and her memorial tower in
   Ireland as contrasted with the Greek hatred for Helen at
   the Scaean Gate.
4, 5, 6. "Moses the Meek" ("Jochanan Hakkadosh") I, II, III,
   1882 [Jocoseria, 1883], exaggerated postscriptal jokes
   about the size of Moses compared to the giant Og.
7. Goldoni, 1883 [Pall Mall Gazette, 1883], graceful tribute
   to a graceful writer of 18th-century Venetian comedy.
8. Rawdon Brown, 1883 [Century, 1884], memorial account of
   an Englishman who found Venice so lovely that he "visited"
   it for forty years.
9. The Founder of the Feast (To Arthur Chappell), 1884 [The
   World, 1884], presentational tribute to the impresario of
   the Popular Saturday and Monday Concerts at St. James's
   Hall.
10. The Names (To Shakespeare), 1884 [Shakespeare Show-Book,
    1884], memorial tribute to a name almost as great as that
    of the ineffable Jehovah, who "didst create us".
11. Why I am a Liberal, c. 1885 [Why I am a Liberal, ed.
    Andrew Reid, 1885], a justification of Liberty as the only
    climate for creative achievement.

From this list certain facts are apparent. Though Browning's
use of the sonnet form extends over a period of fifty years,
almost his entire poetic career, all but three were written in
the 1880's, after his major work was completed. Thus the
sonnets belong to his apprentice years and to his years of decline
To see something of the evolution of his sonnet style one need
only place "Eyes Calm Beside Thee" next to "Rawdon Brown". (5)

SONNET

Eyes, calm beside thee, (Lady couldst thou know!)
　　May turn away thick with fast-gathering tears:
I glance not where all gaze: thrilling and low
　　Their passionate praises reach thee — my cheek wears
Alone no wonder when thou passest by;
Thy tremulous lids bent and suffused reply
To the irrepressible homage which doth glow
　　On every lip but mine: if in thine ears
Their accents linger — and thou dost recall
　　Me as I stood, still, guarded, very pale,
Beside each votarist whose lighted brow
Wore worship like an aureole, 'O'er them all
　　My beauty', thou wilt murmur, 'did prevail
Save that one only: ' — Lady couldst thou know!

RAWDON BROWN

　　"Tutti ga i so gusti, e mi go i mii". <u>Venetian Saying</u>

Sighed Rawdon Brown: "Yes, I'm departing, Toni!
　　I needs must, just this once before I die,
　　Revisit England: <u>Anglus</u> Brown am I,
Although my heart's Venetian. Yes, old crony —
Venice and London — London's 'Death the bony'
　　Compared with Life — that's Venice! What a sky,
　　A sea, this morning! One last look! Good-by,
Cà Pesaro! No, lion — I'm a coney
To weep! I'm dazzled; 'tis that sun I view
　　Rippling the — the — Cospetto, Toni! Down
　　With Carpet-bag, and off with valise-straps!
<u>'Bella Venezia, non ti lascio più!'</u>"
　　Nor did Brown ever leave her: well, perhaps
Browning, next week, may find himself quite Brown!(6)

The first is a typical sonnet from an adoring lover who cannot
tell his Lady how his calm eyes belie his feelings for her: "Lady,
couldst thou know!" Though Browning's delight in drama is in
brief evidence in lines 12, 13, and 14 when the Lady's own words
are hazarded, the spirit of the sonnet is that of the prostrate
lover of the Renaissance — the kind of attitude that Meredith's

hero in <u>Modern Love</u> sarcastically castigates, Browning's <u>Pauline</u>-like hero anticipates, when he describes other lovers and imagines the Lady's own words, the dramatic shorthand of character and place that is later fully evident in the second sonnet that is a little "parleying" with "Rawdon Brown". The "Yes, I'm departing, Toni" of the first line sharply delineates Brown's vignette of conversation with his valet Toni as he plans to depart for London. He looks out at Venice's "What a sky"; but he ends by ordering "Down with carpet-bag, and off with valise straps!" Browning concludes the Petrarchan sonnet with lines that break the mood in Shakespearean fashion, pun on his own name and warn his hostess, Mrs. Bronson (who had suggested the subject matter and requested the poem), that he may linger like Brown — even die himself in Venice. In this poem Browning reveals how he could make the sonnet a vehicle as dramatically unique as his longer monologues.

Different in style and tone is the "Goldoni" sonnet. In the graceful charm of its strict Petrarchan form it recalls in miniature the Venetian elegance of "A Toccata of Galuppi's" — a recollection Browning probably intended since Galuppi wrote music for many of Goldoni's libretti.

GOLDONI

Goldoni — Good, gay, sunniest of souls, —
   Glassing half Venice in that verse of thine —
   What though it just reflect the shade and shine
Of common life, nor render, as it rolls,
Grandeur and gloom? Sufficient for thy shoals
   Was Carnival: Parini's depths enshrine
   Secrets unsuited to that opaline
Surface of things which laughs along thy scrolls.
There throng the people: how they come and go,
   Lisp the soft language, flaunt the bright garb — see —
On Piazza, Calle, under Portico
   And over Bridge! Dear king of Comedy,
Be honored! thou that didst love Venice so,
   Venice, and we who love her, all love thee!

These three examples, along with the quiet elegance of "Helen's Tower" and the straightforward lines of "Why I Am a Liberal" —

"Why?" Because all I haply can and do,
All that I am now, all I hope to be —
. . . .
That little is achieved through Liberty

come near to negating Hatcher's opinion that "Browning's genius
was not at home in the rigid limits of such a fixed form as the
sonnet". (7)

A second apparent observation is that with the possible exception of "Eyes Calm Beside Thee"(8) all Browning's sonnets are
occasional poems: the Marquis of Dufferin and Ava requests a
poem honoring his mother, the granddaughter of Sheridan; the
Goldoni Committee wishes to honor the "king of Comedy"; seeing
the ease with which Browning complies with that request, his
Venetian hostess, Mrs. Bronson, asks a poem for herself about
a contemporary Venetian who has just died, Rawdon Brown. And
so it goes: the presentation album for Arthur Chappell, the
Hospital for Women in Fulham Road and their Shakespearean
Show-Book, Andrew Reid and his anthology for the Liberal Party.
Even the sequence "Moses the Meek", appended to the "Note" to
"Jochanan Hakkadosh", is occasioned by Browning's own wry
after-hope to lend Talmudic mystification and exaggeration to
what DeVane calls an "otherwise bald and unconvincing narrative".
(9) The occasion of the Zappi translation about Michelangelo's
Moses is not known, but with the MS., found among the papers
of George Smith, Browning's publisher and friend, was the note
"From Zappi, R.B. (Given to Ba 'for love's sake', Siena. Sept.
27. '50)". (10) Could it be that this sonnet is a peace offering for
having "said something against putting one's loves into Verse"
and thus discouraging Elizabeth from showing Robert her sonnets
about him until 1849, three years after they were written? It
was at Lucca, he told Miss Wedgwood, a "strange, heavy crown,
that wreath of Sonnets [was] put on me one morning unawares". (11)
Could it be that a year later on their summer sojourn to Siena
Robert made of the Zappi poem an "occasional" presentation to
attest at least his toleration of the sonnet form? If this supposition
and that of Griffin and Minchin about the first sonnet's being
addressed to Eliza Flower contain any truth, then all Browning's
sonnets may rightly be called "occasional". Certainly all were
presented to some person, committee, or "occasional" anthology
or album. To be sure, many sonnets by many poets have been and
will be occasional — but there is a difference with Browning's.

Milton's "Avenge, O Lord Thy Slaughtered Saints", for example, was occasioned by the April 1655 "massacher in Piemont". The letters that Milton as Latin Secretary wrote for Cromwell's signature as well as the subscription for the refugees, to which the poet contributed £ 2, 000, were direct occasional actions. (12) The sonnet was written to vent his personal feeling after he had executed professional and public duties. Browning's sonnets, on the other hand, were written to order, on the request of a person or committee. And perhaps because they were in this case ordered "merchandise", Browning never collected or republished them. Even "Eyes Calm Beside Thee" was signed Z and placed in The Monthly Repository, where Miss Flower would be sure to see it and know its real author. And the "Moses" sequence in "Jochanan Hakkadosh" was occasioned by the poet as annotator and critic in his desire to bolster the tone of the humor of his poem, and "given" to the curious reader in very small print.

This literal sense of scrupulosity may, according to DeVane, have prevented Browning from collecting "his most successful sonnet", "Helen's Tower", (13) as Tennyson did a poem on the same subject in Tiresias and Other Poems (1885). This same attitude on the part of Browning seems to be true for the equally successful "Rawdon Brown" — it belonged to his hostess, Mrs. Bronson. And when she asked his permission to publish it, Browning granted the request. But he was, for the same reason, horrified when Longfellow's daughter Edith published, in the Century Magazine without his permission, the ten lines, "Thus I Wrote in London, Musing on My Betters", which he had written in her album after copying out his little poem, "Touch Him Ne'er So Lightly". For Browning there was a consistency in this view, and it was different from the situation of "The Pied Piper", which he wrote for little Willie Macready to illustrate while the child was ill. The idea for this presentation poem was Browning's, not the Macreadys'. Therefore, while Willie could and did illustrate the poem, Browning could and did publish it in Dramatic Lyrics. (14)

A third observation is that for a prolific poet Browning wrote extremely few sonnets and these few not in the self-revelatory tradition of Shakespeare, Keats, Mrs. Browning, Meredith, and Rossetti. Yet Browning does "sonnet-sing" about himself more than he perhaps intends, just as his men and women are not always entirely dramatis personae. The very fact that Browning chose to respond to these particular "occasional" requests and not to

others that came his way is somewhat indicative of the tastes of
the man. He is, for example, flattered by the request from the
Marquis of Dufferin and Ava; as a dramatist himself he has
genuine interest in Goldoni; as a lover of Venice he sees something of himself in Brown (he even puns on their names and fore-
casts his own death in Venice); as a good amateur musician and
concert goer he can with grace send a tribute to one of the great
impresarios of London; and Shakespeare had always been for him
the archetype of the best and greatest of the "objective" poets.
In fact, the subject matter of these <u>objective</u> occasional poems
furnishes an adequate portrait of Browning the man: a shy young
lover, an exalter of women, one who has interest in Italian artists,
a lover of jokes and ironies, an admirer of Venice, a lover of
drama and music, an idolator of Shakespeare, and a political
liberal. To this extent Browning did "sonnet-sing you about myself".

On the other hand, none of these sonnets is revelatory of strong
emotions in the way that a poet through art transmutes an autobiographical crisis into great poetry. In fact, in the short poem
"House" Browning gives direct, dramatic expression to the same
sort of attitude he had expressed years earlier to E.B.B. after
their marriage — when he "happened early to say something
against putting one's loves in verse". And whatever that <u>some-
thing</u> was, it prevented her from showing him her sonnets for
about three years. Doubtless, the opinion was close to that expressed in "house" with its point of departure an attack on
Wordsworth's "Scorn Not the Sonnet": "'Unlock my heart with
a sonnet-key?'" The controlling image of the poem is a house
whose front walls have been knocked down by an earthquake,
revealing the interior and the domestic habits of its occupant.
For Browning it is not a sonnet-key but a natural disaster that
opens his house to view. Even if the great Shakespeare was
willing thus to "unlock his heart", "the less Shakespeare he!"
The poem is an aspect of the general theme of the entire
<u>Pacchiarotto</u> volume (1886), where it was first published: the
right of privacy. It belongs to the years of Browning's imagined
quarrel with the "British Public, ye who like me not". But
DeVane is doubtless right when he says that "something more
immediate than Wordsworth's sonnet impelled Browning to write
'House'". In 1870 he read the fifty sonnets that then composed
"<u>Sonnets and Songs</u> Toward a Work to be called 'The House of
Life'", a few of which had literally been dug from the grave of

Rossetti's wife, where they had impulsively been buried along
with other poems like "Jenny". Though Browning rather liked
Rossetti, whom he first met in 1855 on one of his London visits,
he apparently felt that the poet-painter had "betrayed the cause
of personal privacy". And in describing "the householder's odd
furniture, musty old books, his exotic and foreign habit of
burning perfumes in his rooms", Browning may have had Rossetti
in mind.(15) The very word House of the title links the poem with
Rossetti, who was long in evolving a suitable title for his sequence, The House of Life. On the other hand, Browning is careful to set this earthquake "in a foreign land" so that the parallel
circumstances would not be exact, just as he had earlier written
of Wordsworth in general terms as "a lost leader" — a reference
he both denied and affirmed. If reading Rossetti's The House of
Life was the immediate cause for Browning's "House", the root
of that cause lay in the fact that "Poor Rossetti" had lost his
wife shortly after the time of Browning's own loss of E.B.B.
Knowing few of the actual conditions of that marriage, Browning
must have seen Rossetti as something of a traitor to the cause
of privacy: not only was he putting his love into verse but into
sonnets — and fleshly ones at that.

Another less immediate cause of "House" may well have been
Meredith's Modern Love. Four months after Mrs. Browning's
death(16) Mary Meredith also died, and Modern Love, which
must have seemed to Browing, as it did to others, a thinly
veiled account of the author's unhappy marriage, made its
appearance in Modern Love and Poems of the English Roadside
(1862). Browning read this volume, but what he really thought
can only be surmised. In typically gallant fashion he compli-
mented the author. Meredith, who was peculiarly sensitive to
unfavorable criticism, was disturbed by the neglect of reviewers'
comments on the chief poem, but he wrote happily to his good
friend, Captain Maxse about Modern Love: "I saw Robert
Browning the other day, and he expressed himself 'astounded
at the originality, delighted with the naturalness and beauty' ".
(17) As for its taste Browning surely must have had his doubts.
Such lines in "House" as

> You see it is proved, what the neighbors guessed:
>   His wife and himself had separate rooms.

could more probably suggest the bedrooms scenes of Modern

<u>Love</u> than the house in Cheyne Walk with its blue china, wombat, and orientalia, where Rossetti moved after his wife's death.

One thing, though, is certain: in 1876 Browning spoke out clearly in "House" against the "confessional" sonnet at a time when he himself was known to have written only two sonnets, translated only one, and published none in a collected volume. And a few years earlier he had written Miss Wedgwood that even the <u>Sonnets from the Portuguese</u> was a heavy burden to him.

In addition to writing very few sonnets and inveighing against the tradition of "putting one's love" into sonnets, Browning allows his numerous <u>men and women</u> to make revealing comments about that form of verse. These references run from <u>Sordello</u> (1840) to "The Two Poets of Croisic" (1878). The three instances from <u>Sordello</u> are of especial interest because Sordello in "Book the Second" wins a troubador's "Court of Love" contest to become the Count's minstrel at Mantua, where rivals like Bocafoli, with his psalms, and Plara, with his sonnets, strive to outdo him:

> The worse,
> That his [Sordello's] poor piece of daily work to do
> Was — not to sink under any rivals; who
> Loudly and long enough, without these qualms,
> Turned, from Bocafoli's stark-naked psalms,
> To Plara's sonnets spoilt by toying with,
> "As knops that stud some almug to the pith
> Pricked for gum, wry thence, and crinkled worse
> Than pursed eyelids of a river-horse
> Sunning himself o'the slime when whirs the breese" —
> (II, 764-773)

> A hungry sun above us, sands that bung
> Our throats, — each dromedary lolls a tongue,
> Each camel churns a sick and frothy chap,
> And you, 'twixt tales of Potiphar's mishap,
> And sonnets on the earliest ass that spoke,
> —Remark, you wonder any one needs choke
> With founts about!   (III, 819-825)

> This town, the minster's trust,
> Held Plara; who, its denizen, bade hail

In twice twelve sonnets, Tempe's dewy vale.
(III, 898-900)(18)

Whether Browning is using the word <u>sonnet</u> in a general sense of
"madrigal" one cannot be sure. Actually the time of Sordello is
almost a century before the fourteen-line sonnet came into being.
But this is shadowy territory at best, and it is not necessary to
assume that Browning speaks anachronistically or accepts a date
other than the first part of the thirteenth century as the most
likely time for the first sonnet. The important point is that he
chose the word <u>sonnet</u> and furnished a four-line example from
Plara in the worst taste of early Renaissance metaphysics. The
semantic note that Browning seems to be striking here is that
the sonnet form is overwritten, over-ornate, dull and trifling in
subject matter, and over-long—twelve sonnets on "Tempe's
dewy vale".

In "Up at a Villa—Down in the City" (1855) the use of the term
is similar. At the city "post-office" the news is always wonder-
fully exciting, thinks "an Italian Person of Quality": notices of
three liberal thieves just shot, the Archbishop's fatherly rebukes
some "little new law" of the Duke

Or a sonnet with flowery marge, to the Reverend Don So-and-S
Who is Dante, Boccaccio, Petrarca, Saint Jerome, and Cicero
"And moreover", (the sonnet goes rhyming,) "the skirts of
Saint Paul has reached,
"Having preached us those six Lent-lectures more unctuous
than ever he preached".

With the mention of Dante, Boccaccio, Petrarca, and the rhyming
process, the speaker seems to refer to a sonnet that tries to
imitate the exaggerated figures of speech of Renaissance sonneteers. Now in the nineteenth century, Browning intimates, that
verse form has fallen into awkward, apprentice hands, and is
attached to the public bulletin board. The semantic implication
is that the sonnet can too easily become an over-flowery, public
thank-you note.

In "One Word More" (1855), which Browning wrote somewhat
hastily after he arrived in London to oversee the publication of
<u>Men and Women</u>, he speaks of the sonnet in his own person, as
he was to do later in "House". The poem was of course a dedication to E.B.B., and somewhat of a public thank-you for the

Sonnets from the Portuguese, now no longer known as "transla-
lations"—if they ever were. The chief point of the poem is that
when one wishes to give a loved one a gift, he gives a unique
one: Dante, for example, painted a picture for Beatrice, and
Rafael "made a century of sonnets" for Margharita. He, Robert
Browning, unfortunately has but one talent, "This of verse,
alone", so he here presents E.B.B. "my fifty men and women".
The interesting point about the use of the term sonnet in this
poem is Browning's insistence that Rafael's gift of sonnets was
right because while the world might view his pictures, "but one
[could view] the volume", that "century of sonnets" now lost to
mankind. Even though Robert's dedicatory "verse alone" must
serve for both public and private gift, the very use of the sonnet
illustration must have made E.B.B. uneasy, wondering if she
had been right in publishing her half-century of sonnets. It is
true that Browning said that he could not reserve to himself "the
finest sonnets written in any language since Shakespeare's", (19)
but the irony of the situation is unmistakable—if unintentional.

The references to the term sonnet in The Ring and the Book
all are chiefly centered around Caponsacchi. In Book I he is "A
prince of sonneteers and lutanists"; the rather coarse narrator
of "Half-Rome" in Book II finds Caponsacchi, like exiled Ovid,
given to "much culture of the sonnet-stave". In Book VI
Caponsacchi himself refers to the process of writing and riming —
"Counting one's fingers till the sonnet's crowned". In Book VII
the sinister Margherita, who believes "All Poetry is difficult to
read", whispers to the swooning Pompilia "Just hear the pretty
verse he [Caponsacchi] made to-day! / A sonnet from Mirtillo,
'Peerless fair. . . .' " In Book IX the garrulous Dr. Bottinius
digresses to describe the admonition that the Law might give to
women like Pompilia "faultless to a fault":

"And dance no more, but fast and pray! avaunt —
"Be burned, thy wicked townsman's sonnet-book!
"Welcome, mild hymnal by. . . some better scribe!"
                                        (IX, 1203-1205)

And in similar vein in Book XI Guido angrily reminds the Abate
Panciatichi of a story about the latter's ancestor when some in-
discreet soul

> —hitched the joke
> Into a sonnet, signed his name thereto,
> And forthwith pinned on post the pleasantry:
> For which he's at the galleys, rowing now
> Up to his waist in water, —just because
> Panciatic and lymphatic rhymed so pat!
> (XI, 1251-1256)

Thus the references to the sonnet by various personages in The Ring tend to fall into one of two definitions: a worthless private love song or canzonet, or a libelous public pasquinade.

In Prince Hohenstiel-Schwangau (1871) the one use of the word sonnet seems merely synonymous with poem and illustrative of the "artistic" drain upon its creator:

> That whoso rhymes a sonnet pays a tax,
> Who paints a landscape dips brush at his cost.
> (lines 1808-1809)

In The Inn Album (1875), however, the use of the term is more integral to the drama about the gambling debts the losing player has scribbled in the margin of the verses in the inn album. The young "polished snob" observes:

> Let's see, however — hand the book, I say!
> Well, you've improved the classic by romance.
> Queer reading! Verse with parenthetic prose —
> 'Hail, calm acclivity, salubrious spot!'
> (Three-two fives) 'life how profitably spent!'
> (Five-nought, five-nine fives) 'yonder humble cot,'
> (More and more noughts and fives) 'in mild content;
> And did my feelings find the natural vent
> Then follow the dread figures—five! 'Content!'
> In friendship and in love, how blest my lot!'
> That's apposite! Are you content as he —
> Simpkin the sonneteer? (I, 128-139)

In the second section of the poem the young man refers again to the words of the Inn-Album sonnet that have come jokingly to stand for the Inn because the countryside itself is "no longer the symbol of natural innocence".(20) By implication the sonnet has become a trite form for trite words:

For see now! — back to 'balmy eminence'
Or 'calm acclivity' or what's the word!
Bestow you there an hour, concoct at ease
A sonnet for the Album, while I put
Bold face on, best foot forward, make for house.
(II, 841–845)

Of note here is the fact that the quoted snatches from one Simpkin
suggest a legitimate sonnet (rather than a general lyric form) by
the meter and rimes, while at the same time the very name of
the poetaster "Simpkin the sonneteer" prefigures and underlines
the pretentious aridity of the verses. Even the dull arithmetic
scratchings in the margins are more engaging. These and other
ironies are woven throughout the long dramatic narrative, which
ends:

" 'Hail, calm acclivity, salubrious spot!'
Open the door!"
No: let the curtain fall!

In "The Two Poets of Croisic" Browning again uses the term
sonnet to denote the petty verses of small poets. René
Gentilhomme, who became a poet of momentary renown by the
accident of prophecy,

Was bound to keep alive the sacred fire,
    And kept it, yielding moderate increase
Of songs and sonnets, madrigals, and much
Rhyming thought poetry and praised as such.
(lines 229–232)

And when his fame died, the world was "saved from more sonneteering". Paul Desforges Maillard, who achieved notoriety by
passing his verses off on Voltaire and La Roque as those of a
feminine-novice, "hoarded" his treasure of "Sonnets and songs
of every size and shape".
    Though it is often difficult in these poems to be sure of the
exact sense of sonnet and sonneteering, one thing is certain:
Browning associates the words with petty poetry and petty poets.
When the score is reckoned up and allowances are made for the
customary uses and denotational changes in the England, France,
and Italy his men and women inhabit, for Browning the term

sonnet implies opprobrium. When he speaks in his own person in "House" or "One Word More", the emphasis is on the impropriety of sonnet-singing about oneself or on the propriety of the private, unpublished sonnets of Rafael's unique gift.

The second conclusion to be drawn from these references is that they occur during the years when Browning himself wrote no sonnets. His 1850 translation of Zappi aside, he wrote "Eyes Calm Beside Thee" in 1834 and "Helen's Tower" in 1870; the other eight sonnets were written in the 1880's. The allusions made by and about his dramatic characters occur from 1840 to 1878. And when Browning decided to use the sonnet for occasiona purposes, his characters ironically make no further mention of that verse form.

The only sonnets Browning published in a collection of his verse were the three in the footnote to "Jochanan Hakkadosh". They form a sequential arrangement indicated by their Roman numerals. The first sonnet recounts Moses' leaping ninety cubits in the air only to discover that he then reached barely to the giant Og's ankle bone. The second sonnet, beginning "And this same fact has met with unbelief!" recounts the speaker's experience walking the length of Og's thigh bone — a four hours' walk. The sonnet ends "respect to Moses, though!" The humor of the second poem, while it can be read and understood separately, is not entirely apparent without the first. Browning emphasizes this unity by beginning the sonnet with And, by referring to Moses' exploit of Sonnet I, and by duplicating the exact Petrarchan rime pattern in both. The third sonnet begins, "Og's thigh bone — if ye deem its measure strange", and goes on to tell of an even strange tale of a stork wading in a "tank" whose bottom has not been reached by a stone that was dropped seventy years ago! Here again the sonnet is intelligible in its own right, but its real point of exaggeration in extremis is lost unless the sequence is read as one poem, though the relationship of the third is not so close as that of the first and second. And the rime scheme with the same octave (abba abba) in all three varies the sestet from cdcdc of I and II to cdecde — in III — just the right shade of riming similarity and difference.

For one who wrote few and disliked the form Browning demonstrates in these sonnets that he is aware of some of the nuances of the sonnet sequence. With his skill in oblique narration one wonders if he were ever tempted to use the techniques of this basically lyric medium to suggest narration by the skill of the juxtaposition of its parts. The truth is that in "James Lee's Wife" Browning actually wrote his sonnet sequence without benefit of sonnets. The poem is a series of dramatic lyrics that tell a story of the marital relations of Mr. and Mrs. Lee. The immediate subject is James Lee — the original title of the poem — and the point of view is strictly that of Mrs. James Lee. Most recent commentators on the poem have begun to see it as somewhat more than another of Browning's dramatic psychological studies. (21) One of the latest of these commentators in "James Lee's Wife' — and Browning's" makes a convincing case for "a remarkable likeness of theme and imagery in 'James Lee's Wife' and Elizabeth's Sonnets from the Portuguese". (22)

An equally good case could be made for "a remarkable likeness" to Meredith's Modern Love. Both poems concern marriages that are falling apart because of too divergent personalities in too exclusively close range of each other. And in each case the woman sacrifices herself — in Modern Love by suicidal poison, in "James Lee's Wife" by fleeing on shipboard. In each poem the point of view is confined — in Modern Love it is the husband who speaks when the omniscience is shifted; in "James Lee's Wife" the wife speaks throughout. Both poems use much nature imagery — a practice unusual for Browning. In fact, it is difficult not to see Meredith's images in

We saw the swallows gathering in the sky,
And in the osier-isle we heard them noise.

   . . .
Love, that had robbed us of immortal things,
This little moment mercifully gave,
Where I have seen across the twilight wave
The swan sail with her young beneath her wings.
     (XLVII, 1, 2, 13-16)(23)

lurking behind Browning's

The swallow has set her six young on the rail,
 And looks sea-ward:
The water's in stripes like a snake, olive-pale
 To the leeward, —
On the weather-side, black, spotted white with the wind.
"Good fortune departs, and disaster's behind", —

> Hark, the wind with its wants and its infinite wail!
>
> (III, 53-60)

Both poets depart from the usual sonnet metrics: Meredith slightly into fifty sixteen-line lyrics, and Browning radically into nine
lyrics of varying lengths and metrics.

There can be little doubt that in the summer of 1862 one of the
books Browning took with him to the coast of Brittany, where
"James Lee's Wife" was primarily written, was Meredith's
Modern Love. (24) It had been published in the spring of that year,
and Browning was curious about the methods both Rossetti and
Meredith were using in writing about the deaths of their wives.
Whether Browning was more influenced by Sonnets from the
Portuguese or Modern Love may be debated. Both of these influ-
ences, however, as well as what Rossetti seemed to be planning
in his songs and sonnets, point to the fact that Browning was
aware of the intriguing possibilities of a sonnet sequence while
at the same time he was determined not to be caught in his
readers' eyes as one who unlocks his heart with a sonnet-key. So
he did two things, both of which were typical Browning procedure
he wrote from the feminine point of view, as he had done in other
poems like "The Glove"; and he transferred some of the features
of the sonnet sequence, like off-stage action and implied narratio
to a sequence of dramatic lyrics — much as Arnold had done in
his "Switzerland" and "Faded Leaves" poems.

Browning's relationship to the sonnet is a series of "satires of
circumstance". Though he wrote no sonnets in his most productiv
middle years, he is the inspirer of the most popular series of the
period. When he spoke ill of putting one's loves into sonnets, Mr.
Browning postponed showing him her sonnets about their love.
After the publication of Sonnets from the Portuguese, when he fel
that some public acknowledgement was due her, he tried thanking
her with the rather hastily written "One Word More". Gallantly
he put his foot in his mouth by praising Rafael for keeping his
sonnets, written to the women he loved best, both private and
unprinted. From 1840 to 1878, when Browning wrote his greatest
poems, his numerous men and women speak surprisingly often
and disparagingly of the sonnet, particularly in The Inn Album.
But when he himself begins to find the sonnet a useful vehicle for
certain occasions, his characters fall silent. Ironically Browning
chooses to record these occasions in the Inn Albums of the world
while an admiring public reads over his now famous shoulder.

Publications in <u>The Shakespeare Show-Book</u>, <u>The Century</u>, <u>Pall-Mall Gazette</u>, <u>The World</u>, and <u>Why I Am a Liberal</u> breached his private prejudice to full public circle. (25)

NOTES

(1) See Dougald MacEachen, "Tennyson and the Sonnet", <u>VN</u>, No. 14 (1958), 1-8 and Footnote 1 in "The Tennysons and the Rossettis: Sonneteering Families".

(2) See the discussion of this matter in "The Nature of the Victorian Sonnet Sequence".

(3) The standard references on this subject state the number as nine (Karl Lentzner, "Robert Browning's Sonettdichtung", <u>Anglia</u>, 9 [1899], 500-17; Harlan H. Hatcher, <u>The Versification of Robert Browning</u> [Columbus: Ohio State Univ. Press, 1928], 132-34). Lentzner did not know of "Eyes Calm Beside Thee" or the Zappi translation; Hatcher does not mention the Zappi, and though he includes "The Founder of the Feast" in his metrical list of sestet rimes, he apparently does not entirely accept the poem as a sonnet even after Browning corrected the original fifteen lines to fourteen (see William C. DeVane, <u>A Browning Handbook</u>, 2nd ed. [New York: Appleton-Century Crofts, 1955], p. 566).

(4) DeVane, p. 470.

(5) Hatcher, p. 133, makes this suggestion, but he does not state how he sees the "evolution".

(6) The text of "Sonnet" is taken from <u>The Complete Works of Robert Browning</u>, ed. Roma A. King, <u>et al</u>, (Athens: Ohio Univ. Press, 1969), I, 57. The text of "Rawdon Brown" is from <u>The Complete Works of Robert Browning</u> (Arno Edition), ed. Charlotte Porter and Helen A. Clarke (New York: George D. Sproul, 1899), XII, 276 (all subsequent quotations from Browning's poems are from this edition unless otherwise noted).

(7) Hatcher, p. 132.

(8) Though information about the composition of this sonnet is not known, Griffin and Minchin (<u>The Life of Robert Browning</u> [London: Methuen, 1938], p. 309) suggest that it was occasioned by Browning's youthful devotion to Eliza Flower.

(9) <u>Handbook</u>, p. 472.

(10) <u>New Poems by Robert Browning and Elizabeth Barret Browning</u>, ed. Sir Frederic G. Kenyon (New York: Macmillan,

1915), p. 26. Probably unknown to Browning, Sir Aubrey de Vere had translated this same sonnet in 1842, "The Statue of Moses: From Zappi".

(11) Robert Browning and Julia Wedgwood: A Broken Friendship as Revealed by Their Letters, ed. Richard Curle (New York: Stokes, 1937), pp. 99-100.

(12) See The Complete Poems of John Milton, ed. F.A. Patterson (New York: Crofts, 1934), p. 55 of "Notes".

(13) Handbook, p. 560.

(14) In a letter to Furnivall, Browning writes, "William Macready oldest boy. . . . asked me to give him some little thing to illustrate; so, I made a bit of a poem out of an old account of the death of the Pope's legate at the Council of Trent" (Letters of Robert Browning, Collected by Thomas J. Wise, ed. T.L. Hood [New Haven: Yale Univ. Press, 1933], p. 197). This poem, "The Cardinal and the Dog", Browning did not publish until his last volume Asolando (1889), mainly at the insistence of the Browning Society; the poem was revised and now in a sense "belonged" again to the poet, for Willie Macready had been dead several years. "The Pied Piper", on the other hand, was an after-thought presented to Willie not in answer to his original request, and therefore "belonged" to them both as, for example, did "One Word More", written for, but certainly not requested by, E.B.B. in 1855.

(15) Handbook, p. 400. See Also DeVane's "The Harlot and the Thoughtful Young Man: A Study of the Relation between Rossetti's Jenny and Browning's Fifine at the Fair", SP 24 (1932), 463-484.

(16) The deaths of the three wives occurred in a space of nine months: E.B.B. in June, 1861; Mary Meredith in October, 1861; and Elizabeth Rossetti in February, 1862.

(17) Letters of George Meredith, ed. by his Son (New York: Scribners, 1912), I, 73.

(18) The first two of these quotations from Sordello (as well as those to follow from other poems) were suggested by L.N. Broughton and B.F. Stetler, A Concordance to the Poems of Robert Browning (New York: Stechert, 1924-25). The third one, "twice twelve sonnets", was apparently overlooked by the editors and it is Browning's most specific reference to the tedium of sonnets in series. (The texts of these quotations are taken from The Works of Robert Browning, ed. F.G. Kenyon, Centenery Edition, 10 vols. London: Smith Elder, 1912.)

(19) Edmund Gosse, Critical Kit-Kats (London: Heinemann, 1896

p. 3. Though Gosse is unreliable in some of his statements about Sonnets from the Portuguese (particularly those having to do with the forged Reading edition), the spirit of this statement attributed to Browning is doubtless true enough. At least Mrs. Browning said much the same thing when she wrote to her sister Arabel on January 12, 1851, that when Robert saw the manuscript of the sonnets, he was "much touched and pleased" and thought so highly of the poetry that he "could not consent that they be lost" to her volumes (quoted from an unpublished letter in the Berg Collection by Gardner B. Taplin, The Life of Elizabeth Barrett Browning [New Haven: Yale Univ. Press, 1957], p. 233).

(20) Roma A. King, Jr., The Focusing Artifice: The Poetry of Robert Browning (Athens: Ohio Univ. Press, 1968), p. 196.

(21) Following the lead of C.H. Herford, Robert Browning (New York, 1905), H.C. Duffin, in Amphibian: A Reconsideration of Browning: A Portrait (London: Bower & Bower, 1962), sees it as connected with the frustration of Robert's and Elizabeth's marriage.

(22) Glenn Sandstrom, VP, 4 (Autumn, 1966), 259-270.

(23) The Works of George Meredith, Memorial Edition, XXIV (New York: Scribners, 1910), p. 227.

(24) DeVane, Handbook, p. 285. Frederic E. Faverty's "Browning's Debt to Meredith in James Lee's Wife" (Essays in American and English Literature Presented to Bruce Robert McElderry, Jr., ed. Max F. Schulz, with William D. Templeman and Charles R. Metzger, [Athens: Ohio Univ. Press, 1967], pp. 290-305) discusses Browning's indebtedness to Meredith in considerable detail. (I was unable to consult Professor Faverty's essay in time for writing this section. Since my argument is similar to his, but with different illustrative statements, I prefer it to stand on its own.)

(25) William Sharp included two of Browning's sonnets ("Helen's Tower" and "Why I Am a Liberal") in his Sonnets of This [Nineteenth] Century (London: Walter Scott, [1886])—a carefully edited collection of 300 sonnets.

4. ARNOLD'S SONNETS

(A)

Though his sonnets, with the exception of two or three, have received scant critical attention, Arnold was the most successful sonneteer among the major Victorian poets before 1865. Tennyson is known to have written fifty-two sonnets, but "as a sonneteer he is, relatively, a failure". (1) Mrs. Browning's single sonnets have never received high praise, and critical evaluation of her popular Sonnets from the Portuguese has varied markedly during the century since its publication. Though he was "The Onlie Begetter" of this series, Browning never liked the sonnet form and is known to have written only eleven. (2) Arnold, on the other hand, is known to have written twenty-nine – a number that is significant when the relatively small body of his total poetic works is considered.

The Strayed Reveller, and Other Poems (1849), Arnold's first volume, opened with the sonnet he later called "Quiet Work"; it remained a kind of foreword in most of his volumes until 1869, and after 1877 it was always first among "Early Poems". Of the remaining twenty-six poems in the first volume, ten were sonnets. While only two new sonnets appeared in the second volume, Empedocles on Etna, and Other Poems (1852), the 1867 volume of New Poems contained fourteen new sonnets among forty-five selections. (3) Numerically, then, about one-third of The Strayed Reveller and New Poems was made up of sonnets. To put the matter still another way, almost one-fourth of Arnold's total published poems is made up of sonnets. (4) Even if it can be argued that the fourteen-line sonnet is too short a poem to be considered the numerical equal of a work like Merope of 2024 lines, it must be remembered that Arnold gave special separate grouping to most of his sonnets in his two most important volumes — The Strayed Reveller and New Poems. (5) And when he came to make the many arrangements and rearrangements of his collected poems, he gave to the sonnets a special category. (6) This ordering is significant because Arnold believed that one of the mistakes Wordsworth had made was in the grouping of his poems: "He has poems of the fancy, poems of the imagination, poems of sentiment and reflection, and so on. His cat-

egories are ingenious but far-fetched, and the result of his
employment of them is unsatisfactory. . . . The tact of the
Greeks in matters of this kind was infallible. . . . Epic, dramatic, lyric, and so forth, have a natural propriety, and should
be adhered to. "(7) In grouping his own poetry Arnold did not
hesitate to list "Sonnets" beside "Narrative Poems", "Lyric
and Elegiac Poems", and "Dramatic and Later Poems" even
though the Greeks did not have a word for sonnet. Thus Arnold
never placed his sonnets to the side as if they were a miscellaneous epilogue of items not quite the equal of the rest of his
poems.

Indeed, Arnold's sonnets occupy so unique a position in the
total body of his poetry that it is the contention of this study
that they both anticipate and summarize most of his major ideas.
With the exception of love, the sonnets are microcosms of
Arnold's poetic themes, just as they also suggest some of the
central concerns of his later prose. In addition, the metrical
patterns of the sonnets underscore his changing attitude toward
versification: in his sonnets and in his longer poems Arnold
moved from metrical experimentation toward more conservative
forms. Though his opinion of the sonnet as a poetic vehicle
seems somewhat ambivalent, Arnold nevertheless created memorable examples that are recognizably Arnoldian by the sustained
landscape of their nature imagery and by a classic simplicity
and balance of phrase and line.

To become aware of the significance of the subject matter of
his sonnets it is necessary to remember that Arnold wrote
almost all his sonnets in two periods twenty years apart, fourteen from 1844 to 1849, and fourteen from 1863 to 1864. (8) The
Lusitania sonnet of 1878, which he never republished, was a
somewhat belated coda and the only sonnet about a member of
his family. The first period corresponds to the most fruitful
time of Arnold's poetic career. The forties saw the composition
of the poems of The Strayed Reveller volume and the beginnings
of "Empedocles", "Tristram", "Obermann", and the Marguerite
poems — the major pieces of the 1852 volume. These were the
years between Oxford and marriage: the years of close friendship with Clough, visits to France and Switzerland, the fellowship at Oriel, and the pleasant duties as secretary to Lord
Lansdowne.

The subject matter of the sonnets of this period is similarly
wide-ranging. Those on Shakespeare, Bishop Butler, Emerson,

and Sophocles announce the literary critic's concern with a
creative writer's understanding of all life, as well as guarding
his personal right of privacy, and the virtues of wholeness and
unity in great spirits who can see "life steadily and see it whole".
Those on Wellington, the Hungarian nation, and "Republican"
Clough concern politics: the need to comprehend the nature of
"the general law" of social progress and to realize that the ideal
day of true Greek liberty will not dawn soon. "In Harmony with
Nature" and "Quiet Work" indicate the lessons man should learn
from Nature before attempting to surpass her. "Religious Isolation" and "To George Cruikshank" underscore Arnold's per -
sonal stoicism, and "Youth's Agitations" and "The World's
Triumphs" further comment on the difficulties of the human con-
dition. Literature, politics, nature, religion, and personal
philosophy—these are the subjects of Arnold's early sonnets;
they are also with the exception of love the subjects of the main
body of his poetry.

Just as the subject matter of the early sonnets is varied, so
is their metrical form. Although five of the fourteen introduce
a third rime in the octave (abba, acca — one of the favorite
patterns of Wordsworth), the dominant structure of these sonnets
is Italian or Petrarchan. Only the two sonnets of the 1852 volume
which were once to be a part of a sequence, are, strictly speaking
English or Shakespearean. In fact, the most striking feature of
this early group is that almost all the major variants of sonnet
structure are represented. "To a Republican Friend, 1848" has
the usual Italian octave abba, abba, while "To the Duke of
Wellington" reproduces the same pattern but on four instead of
two sounds: abba, cddc. And the "Sonnet to the Hungarian Nation"
keeps the two rime sounds but in the variant order of abba, baab.
Not only is the Wordsworthian octave well represented, but so is
the Miltonic device of having the break in thought and grammatic
structure other than at the end of the eighth line. The major
division of thought in the "Butler" sonnet occurs after the first
quatrain, and in the familiar "saw life steadily and saw it whole"
sonnet ("To a Friend") the major division comes at the end of
the first line. Thus the whole gamut of the sonnet in English —
in its major metrical phases: variants on the Italian, Miltonic,
Wordsworthian, and Shakespearean — is represented in these
early sonnets.

Quite the opposite is true of the sonnets that Arnold wrote
after 1853. Of the fourteen written in 1863 and 1864 all conform

to the accepted octave pattern of the strict Italian sonnet: abba, abba. And the variations in the sestets are those usually found in Italian sonnets of the Renaissance. (9) Even the occasional shifting of the traditional break in thought after the eighth line had long been sanctioned by Milton's use.

What had happened to Arnold as poet and person during the intervening years between 1850 and the summer of 1863 when he apparently wrote ten of his last fourteen sonnets? He had abandoned Marguerite or the image of pert charm for which she was perhaps a symbol; he had married Frances Lucy Wightman, daughter of Sir William Wightman, Justice of the Queen's Bench. He had forsaken the rather glamorous world of private secretary to the Marquis of Lansdowne, Lord President of the Council, to become an Inspector of Schools. He had begun to turn from poetry to prose criticism. Instead of new poems Arnold produced new arrangements and editions. "Sohrab and Rustum" is substituted for "Empedocles on Etna", and "Balder Dead" is the chief new adornment of Poems, Second Series (1855). He had become Professor of Poetry at Oxford and had begun his thesis that Homer and the Greeks are modern in spirit and simple in style and almost alone worthy of serious imitation. He had traveled to Switzerland again, this time with his wife; and he had stood on the terrace at Berne and imagined Marguerite

> long since wandered back,
> Daughter of France! to France, thy home;
> And flitted down the flowery track
> Where feet like thine too lightly come.

In Paris he no longer wished to see George Sand; he wanted to meet Sainte-Beuve.

In 1863 Arnold wrote to his mother, who apparently liked the "true feeling" she found in Jean Ingelow's poetry: "I do not at present very much care for poetry unless it can give me true thought as well". (10) In this spirit of tranquillity "certain of these sonnets were composed on Sundays in the summer of 1863. No less than ten entries in the note-books relating to this group [of fourteen] are found between June 21 and August 25. "(11) He looks back, for example, to his impressions of the actress Rachel when he was a visiting undergraduate in Paris, or he records his true thought from the reading he is doing for his essays and lectures.

Indeed the major portion of the subject matter of these fourteen sonnets comes from his reading and study: Barréra's
Memoirs of Rachel (1858), Marcus Aurelius, Morison's The Life
and Times of St. Bernard (1863), Ozanam's Les Poètes
franciscains en Italie au treizième siècle (1852), and St.
Augustine's Confessions. These sonnets illustrate "how difficult
[Arnold] found it to write poetry after 1860". (12) Yet they are
small examples of the cast of mind that is peculiarly Arnoldian —
the blend of objective and subjective that when rightly achieved
produced some of his best poetry. Though he follows Barréra's
Memoirs accurately in the details of the "Rachel" sequence,
Arnold makes the climax of the first and best sonnet peculiarly
personal:

Ah, where the spirit its highest life hath led
All spots, matched with that spot, are less divine;
And Rachel's Switzerland, her Rhine, is here.

The sonnet becomes, as M. Bonnerot has suggested, an allusion
to Arnold's own past: the Switzerland of Marguerite and the Rhine
journey where he followed in the wake of Frances Lucy. (13) Personal allusiveness — this time to his relationships with his father -
is the same sort of thing on a larger scale that keeps "Sohrab and
Rustum" from being as flat as "Balder Dead". Similarly, when
Arnold visits the ancestral home of the Byron family and reads in
some guidebook about the painting that preserves the legend of the
striking of a son senseless, he thinks as son and father that this
violent act is far more tragic than "Byron's woe". And as literary
critic Arnold doubtless recalls his opinion of Byron in "Memorial
Verses" that he "Taught us little; but our soul / Had felt him like
the thunder's roll". Also as literary critic when Arnold reads in
Ozanam the incident of the death of the young wife of Giacopone
di Todi, he sees in her wearing of sackcloth beneath her gorgeous
gown a lesson for poets: "a hidden ground / Of thought and of
austerity within" — a philosophical belief he had long held and
expressed in letters to his mother, in essays and lectures, and
in such poems as "The Strayed Reveller" and "Resignation".
For Arnold great poetry must not be merely a sick romanticism
"that infects the world" with its gorgeously deceptive surface.
    Not all of these latter sonnets reflect Arnold's reading. "East
London" and "West London", a complementary pair about the
city's poor, indicate the personal attitude of a busy school inspec-

tor who met and talked with the Rev. William Tyler in the East
End (where "the mortality was twice as great . . . as in the
West End")(14) and who also saw the poor in Belgrave Square
when he kept social engagements there. About the time of composing these sonnets Arnold wrote to Lady de Rothschild: "I
should like to meet, but it is not easy to escape from my
devouring schools, even for a day. " And a little later: "Again
and again I have meant to come . . . but I just get here, within
reach of the Belgravian paradise, when I am swept back again
into the outer darkness of Fenchurch Street. "(15) "Immortality"
likewise represents a personal restatement of ideas expressed
to Clough as early as 1848 and later in lines from "Rugby Chapel"
(16); its main theme is that we cannot give in to the "brutal world",
for only he "who flagged not in the earthly strife" mounts to
eternal life. And the legend of "East and West" is apparently the
result of Arnold's 1863 visit to Wales rather than of his reading.

The subject matter of these latter sonnets, whether from personal experience or from reading, represents the main directions
of Arnold's mature thinking. In the "Rachel" sonnets, when he
returns to the favorite actress of his earlier years, he sees her
not only as a symbol of past personal memories but also of the
general "eclectic nature of Western culture":(17)

Germany, France, Christ, Moses, Athens, Rome.
The strife, the mixture in her soul, are ours.

This sonnet is the seed for the dualism discussed in the famous
chapter "Hebraism and Hellenism" in Culture and Anarchy (1869).
In addition to evidence of social criticism in this sonnet and in
"East London" and "West London", the majority of the later
sonnets show Arnold's interest in the religious-ethical criticism
that later appeared in his articles on St. Paul in Cornhill (1869)
and culminated in Literature and Dogma (1873) and God and the
Bible (1875). Many of the sonnets of 1863-1864 anticipate this
interest just as they indicate Arnold's reading and thinking. "The
Better Part" is to emulate Christ, whether he is divine or human,
and to obey "the inward judge". "Immortality", as has been stated,
is only for those "who flagged not in the earthly strife". "The
Divinity" maintains with St. Bernard that "Wisdom and goodness,
they are God!" And "The Good Shepherd with the Kid" and "Monica's
Last Prayer" recount two ennobling legends of the early Christians.
The subject matter of both the early and late groups of sonnets

has one thing in common: Arnold's interest in literary criticism continues from "Shakespeare" (1849) to "Austerity of Poetry" (1867). This interest is but earnest of Arnold's passion for prose criticism that continues from <u>On Translating Homer</u> (1861) to <u>Essays in Criticism</u> (1865, 1888) to <u>Mixed Essays</u> (1879) and <u>Irish Essays and Others</u> (1882). There is, however, one theme new to the latter group. Two of its sonnets — the first and last by their dates of composition — reflect the domestic scene, a theme that is absent from the early sonnets. In "A Picture at Newstead" (written in June, 1863) Arnold finds the "woe" of his old whipping-boy Byron to be far less genuinely tragic than the "dumb remorse" of that Lord Arundel who struck senseless his son. In his last sonnet, "S. S. 'Lusitania'" (written in December, 1878), Arnold, while reading Dante on the death of Ulysses off Teneriffe, thinks what dangers the Australian voyage (that takes part of the same route) may hold for his only surviving son, Richard Penrose. So is it with the main body of Arnold's verse. The brief glimpses of personal domesticity that are intimated in "Resignation" and "Tristram and Iseult" find central expression in "Rugby Chapel", "Stanzas from Carnac", and the elegies to the family pets — Geist, Mathias, and Kaiser.

This Arnoldian domesticity tends increasingly to be cast in the elegiac mold. "Memorial Verses: April, 1850" was written at the request of the Wordsworth family. But by April, 1855, in "Haworth Churchyard" Arnold had "buried" poor Harriet Martineau twenty years before her time. Just so in his last sonnet he foreshadowed his son's death and, albeit unknowingly, the tragic end of the ship <u>Lusitania</u>. So strongly had the elegiac cast of thinking been growing in Arnold's poetry that when in 1869 he experimented with classifying his poems as "Narrative and Elegiac" and "Dramatic and Lyric" — without his usual "Sonnet" category — he placed only one of his early sonnets, "Shakespeare", in the "Elegiac" section whereas four of the later group were so placed: "A Picture at Newstead" and the three "Rachel" sonnets.

Thus the subject matter of the entire twenty-nine sonnets represents the main interests of Arnold: from a variety of early concerns with politics, nature, and the origin and meaning of poetry to a more restrained concern with the critical verities of family, social, and religious ethics. Only <u>love</u>, the traditional theme of sonneteers from Shakespeare to Mrs. Browning to John Berryman, is absent from Arnold's sonnets. It seems strange that during the years when Arnold was writing his best poems about love in the "Switzerland" and "Faded Leaves" groupings and in "Tristram and Iseult" he wrote no sonnet cycle and no love sonnet. Yet even here there is an affinity with the sonnet. G. Robert Stange suggests that "Switzerland" might be regarded as a nineteenth-century equivalent of the Elizabethan sonnet cycles". (18)

Two questions, however, Professor Stange leaves unanswered: Did Arnold think in terms of sonnet groupings? What was his opinion of Elizabethan verse conventions?

The answer to the first question is "yes". As has already been intimated in discussing the subject matter of the sonnets, Arnold often projected his train of thought beyond the first fourteen lines. In "To a Republican Friend", for example, he begins by defining his meaning of liberal revolution, and then in "Continued", which begins with the word Yet, he reminds "Republican" Clough that the swift action in France may not suddenly bring in the ideal day. "Religious Isolation: To the Same" is connected to the preceding two at least by its title, and certainly it is closely related to this Republican friend who had just resigned his Oriel fellowship and who needed a greater degree of what Arnold elsewhere calls self-dependence (the adjective "Religious" being used in the broad sense of philosophical). In fact, the familiar "Sonnet: To a Friend", beginning with the awkward line "Who prop, thou ask'st, in these bad days, my mind?" was also written to Clough and is thematically associated with the other three even though Arnold separated it from the others in the first volume to provide a stoical equipoise between "Mycerinus" and "The Strayed Reveller". These four sonnets to Clough, then, are a good example of the kind of meditative series that Arnold's spiritual godfather Wordsworth was fond of writing — Personal Talk, for instance, also contains four sonnets.

"Written in Butler's Sermons" and "Written in Emerson's Essays", placed side by side in the 1849 volume with parallel titles and similarly rimed octaves, are clearly meant as a contrasting pair of "undergraduate" sonnets. In the Spasmodic style and "manner of the Madman", they link the hero Emerson and antihero Butler in the poet's cry for recognition of individual human dignity. (19) Two other groupings, moreover — one finished and one unfinished — indicate beyond doubt that Arnold gave thought to sequential sonnet arrangements. The only two sonnets of the 1852 volume, in which the majority of the "Switzerland" and "Faded Leaves" poems first appeared, are the sole survivors of a projected group of five, Shakespearean in theme and style. The Yale MS list of poems to be composed in 1849 identifies "The World's Triumphs" and "Youth's Agitations" as the second and third members of the group: "5 sonnets — out thunder — So far ['The World's Triumphs'] — When I have found ['Youth's Agitations'] . —"(20) The other three were either not written or discarded. The finished sequence, the most positive evidence of Arnold's concern with grouping, is of course the three "Rachel sonnets, labeled I, II, III with no additional individual titles. The narrative movement of the sequence is Rachel ill, Rachel dying, Rachel dead and immortal. Even though the sonnets were not written until 1863, Arnold's devotion to the great French tragedienne went back to 1847, when he was first moved by her "intellectual power". And it was between these years of 1847 and 1863 that Arnold was writing, arranging, and rearranging the love poems of "Switzerland" and "Faded Leaves". Having past models from the Elizabethan poets as well as Mrs. Browning's Sonnets from the Portuguese and having experimented with various patterns of sonnet grouping, Arnold seems to have deliberately chosen to avoid the sonnet form for his love poems.

The answer to the second question — What was Arnold's opinion of Elizabethan poetry? — sheds light on this avoidance of the love sonnet. Arnold usually gave lip service to the greatness of the Elizabethans, but "whenever he amplified a reference it became an inquiry into their shortcomings". (21) Presumably the elaborate style of Raleigh as opposed to the simple elegance of Thucydides goes for sonneteering too. (22) Long ago Stuart Pratt Sherman assessed Arnold and the Elizabethans: "One is almost tempted to suggest that in 'getting up' the [Elizabethan] Period he selected Spenser and Shakespeare as its best representatives and let the rest go. "(23) Yet Professor E. K. Brown finds that "From Dryden down no critic of anything like Arnold's rank has said so little of Shakespeare". (24) Neither Sherman nor Brown had the benefit of Arnold's Note-books nor his frank remarks to Clough. From the Note-books it seems that Arnold had some difficulty finding time to read Shakespeare's sonnets — at least they do not get checked off as quickly as other items. (25) To Clough he remarked disparagingly of poets who have a "desire of fullness without respect of the means. . . . yes and those d----d Elizabethan poets generally. Those who cannot read G[ree]k sh[ou]ld read nothing but Milton and parts of Wordsworth: the state should see to it. "(2

All of these hints of an attitude toward Elizabethan style and verse suggest why Arnold did not wish to follow in the tradition of the Elizabethan sonnet series. After all, this was not a classic form, nor was it a modern form that lent itself to classic simplicity. In fact, the subjects of Arnold's own sonnets would indicate that he saw Milton and Wordsworth as the only worthy sonneteers, perhaps because they had broadened the scope of the sonnet's subject matter. In short, Arnold seems to have wished to disassociate his poetry from the Elizabethan sonnet series of love and to experiment with a Miltonic-Wordsworthian sonnet. For his love poems in "Switzerland" and "Faded Leaves" he seems to prefer for a model the German Liedercyklus. (27) He even urges Clough, who seems to have had an early passion for the sonnet, to give over the form along with his "Drat" hexameters. (28) "Try a bit in the metre I took for the sick king", he advises in 1849. (29) So strong is Arnold's feeling during the 1840's for experiments in original or partly original verse forms, along with his "classic" subject matter, that it is rather surprising he wrote any sonnets at all, to say nothing of his three best sonnets.

(B)

Just as the subject matter of Arnold's sonnets, with the exception of love, represents the main interests of his poetry and prose, so does the patterning of his experimentation with sonnet structure correspond to his attitudes toward versification. The great variety in the metrics of his early sonnets, as previously noted, corresponds to a similar variety in the versification of the 1849 volume. Almost every poem is in a different verse form, "The Strayed Reveller" explores the infinite variety of free verse, and "Mycerinus" uses the dramatic contrast of a Spasmodic five-line stanza with a limpid blank verse. "Tristram and Iseult", begun in 1848 but not published until 1852, has each of its three parts in a different but structurally appropriate verse form. On the other hand, the rather strict Petrarchan forms of the later sonnets correspond closely to Arnold's more conservative tastes for the blank verse of "Sohrab and Rustum", "Balder Dead", and Merope. Even the partially original verse forms of "Obermann" and "The Scholar-Gipsy" find themselves repeated in "Obermann Once More" and "Thyrsis". Though it cannot be said as H. C. Duffin puts it, "All [of Arnold's sonnets] are in the Petrarchan form, with the Wordsworthian variation in lines 6 and 7", (30) it can be said that Arnold preferred Petrarchan principles, but with wide latitude and great variety. In his most

familiar sonnet, "Shakespeare", for example, the sestet rime
dedeff gives the ear the effect of a quatrain and couplet—a
Shakespearean pattern, which after 1869 Arnold disguised for
the eye by having it printed as two tercets. And the d rime know
is an eye rime for the f's, bow and brow. (31) Arnold thus keeps
two rime patterns going at the same time so that his own
Petrarchan thought structure ends in Shakespearean homage.

Skillful effects of this sort inevitably pose the question of the
poetic quality of Arnold's sonnets as poems. While few of
Arnold's major critics have judged his sonnets to contain his
best poetry, they have found some to admire. The critic not
familiar with some of Arnold's techniques often judges a sonnet
poor for strange or wrong reasons. William Michael Rossetti
in reviewing "To George Cruikshank" for the Germ, objected to
the conventional eighteenth-century diction of "breathless glades"
and "shy Dian's horn" without suspecting that Arnold was indirectly making a point about "the efficacy of eighteenth-century
pastoral when it comes to coping with moral issues of the soul".
(32) F. R. Leavis's intemperate attack on "Shakespeare" for
"the vagueness of the idea" is based on the false assumption
that Arnold is "a versifier in the Romantic tradition (and a
Wordsworthian)". (33) Leavis, therefore, fails to see even the
simple link between "the loftiest Hill" and Shakespeare's
"victorious brow".

More judicial critics have in the main found Arnold's sonnets
pleasant, with occasional memorable lines. Even the exacting
Saintsbury speaks well of the later sonnets, none of which

> equals Shakespeare; and one may legitimately hold the
> opinion that the sonnet was not specially Mr. Arnold's
> form. Its greatest examples have always been reached
> by the reflex, the almost combative, action of intense
> poetic feeling—Shakespeare's, Milton's, Wordsworth's,
> Rossetti's—and intensity was not Mr. Arnold's charac-
> teristic. Yet Austerity of Poetry, East London, and
> Monica's Last Prayer must stand so high in the second
> class that it is hardly critical weakness to allow them the
> first. (34)

An equally exacting modern critic-scholar, Paull F. Baum, who
finds Arnold wanting in greatness in several of his major poems,
devotes an entire essay to "Shakespeare", which he finds "has a

general unity, and if it is not what we expected Arnold to say, the
fault may possibly be our own".(35) Baum's essay is an eloquent
answer to those, like Leavis, who fail to see that Arnold's best
poems — "Dover Beach", for instance — can be read in several
ways.(36) This sonnet is an example of Arnold's belief that
"classic" subjects generalized with care can be lastingly meaningful — a point Arnold argued often with Clough. While there is an
obvious need for more informed and detailed studies of Arnold's
individual sonnets, the bulk of opinion contemporary to Arnold
and that of the present time would in the main agree that the
sonnets are indeed poems in their own rights.(37)

(C)

Though there is not an Arnoldian sonnet in the sense that there
is a Miltonic sonnet — with its characteristic organlike unity — or
even a Wordsworthian sonnet with its third rime sound in the
Petrarchan octave — the best of Arnold's sonnets are clearly
recognizable by the landscape of their nature imagery. Unlike
Elizabethan sonnet imagery, Arnold's is usually simple yet inter-
woven beyond the sonnet's customary figures of speech. In the
familiar "Shakespeare" the central image of "the loftiest hill"
extends to five and one-half lines of the octave, but the visual
aspects are uncomplicated: the hill is high, uncrowning itself
only to the stars, revealing to men only its "cloudy border",
firmly anchored in the sea. Thus aspects of heaven, earth, and
the depths beneath — cosmological, biological, and geological
concepts — are all present in the great mountain and in the greater
writer Shakespeare. The intricacy of Arnold's imagery lies
rather in the interweaving of the metaphor with its idea of
Shakespeare himself, who in the opening lines is "free" and "out-
topping" — adjectives that anticipate the mountain free of clouds
only at its out-topping crest. In the sestet Shakespeare, like the
mountain, "didst the stars and sunbeams know". And the final
image of the "victorious brow" recalls the lofty hill.
Another example of his organic use of landscape occurs in
"Written in Butler's Sermons". Here Arnold is lamenting in the
octave Bishop Butler's logic-chopping of man's "Affections,
Instincts . . . Impulse and Reason" into "a thousand shreds"
when actually these human phenomena are quite interdependent.
In the sestet man's unified being reveals itself

> . . . like sister-islands seen
> Linking their coral arms under the sea.
> Or clustered peaks with plunging gulfs between
> Spanned by aerial arches all of gold,
> Where'er the chariot wheels of life are rolled
> In cloudy circles to eternity.

Thus the interlocking worlds of sea, land, air, and rainbow
figuratively convey Arnold's meaning of spiritual and psychic
unity, especially as contrasted with the flat absence of images
in the octave.

Occasionally Arnold reverses his landscape imagery into a
negative arrangement; that is, he leaves his major theme pur-
posefully unadorned, confining the figurative language to the
idea he wishes to contravene. In "To George Cruikshank", for
example, Arnold asks what should men "to middle fortune born",
do when they see the artist's terrifying engravings of drunken-
ness? Should they retreat to Nature: to "breathless glades,
cheered by shy Dian's horn" or to "cold-bubbling springs, or
caves"? These images Arnold means to be negative because they
are trite in pattern and overblown in diction. They contrast
sharply with the Stoic brevity of the positive point of the sonnet:
"Not so! The Soul / Breasts her own griefs". Man must recog-
nize the worst if he is to fight it intellectually; he must not run
to weary Nature with his man-made problems: "Know thou the
worst! So much, not more, he can." Arnold makes his point
here expositorily and meditatively in the tradition of sonneteers,
but he also underlines it by a negative nature imagery.

An example of the economical use of nature imagery in both
the negative and positive senses occurs in the first Rachel sonnet. In the octave the images all concern heat - the furnace of
cities: "Sere, in the garden of the Tuileries, / Sere with
September drooped the chestnut trees". In the sestet Arnold
asks why the worn and ill Rachel stops "by this empty play-
house drear". The answer is that "Rachel's Switzerland, her
Rhine, is here!" These positive, personal symbols of mountains
and water that represent ideality to Arnold are transferred in
economical fashion to the actress Rachel, with whose intellectual
acting the poet felt an especial affinity.

This landscape of Arnold's with its mountains, islands, glades,
and rivers is not unique to him nor limited to his sonnets. Indeed,
A. Dwight Culler in Imaginative Reason: The Poetry of Matthew
Arnold sees the poet's insistent use of these almost trite images

as the key to what is called, in the opening chapter, "The World of the Poems": "the Forest Glade, the Burning or Darkling Plain, and the Wide Glimmering Sea". What is unique in the sonnets is the variety of the use of this imagery. Since the Italian sonnet — Arnold's favorite pattern — is composed of two parts, the octave and the sestet, Arnold's various plans of adornment are what mark and make his sonnets unique. Among the examples just cited, in "Shakespeare" the loftiest hill symbolizes the positive idea of the bard's inexhaustible variety; the negative idea of the critics' biographical probing is left without imagery. In the Butler sonnet the positive idea of spiritual unity is elaborately configured as opposed to the drab statement of Butler's notion of the complete separateness of man's "Affections, Instincts . . . Impulses and Reason". And in the first Rachel sonnet Arnold makes the negative octave a simple description of Paris in August as his torrid Burning Plain and the sestet, his cool mountains and river: Switzerland and the Rhine, which are laden with implied biographical imagery for both himself and Rachel.

When Arnold can find no way to make integral these features of his natural world, his sonnets are largely failures. "Worldly Place" is an illustration of this failure. The octave, opening with a paraphrase from Marcus Aurelius, "<u>Even in a palace, life may be led well</u>", makes the point that the common life of man is a "stifling den", where freedom is sold to please a "foolish master's ken". The sestet consoles the reader with the remembrance of Aurelius's words that palaces are no better: "'There were no succour here! / The aids to noble life are all within'". The idea and the structure of the sonnet are impeccable, but when the Arnoldian landscape is missing, the sonnet itself is scarcely poetry.

A similarly prosy sonnet, "The Divinity" — based on St. Bernard's idea that "<u>Wisdom and goodness, they are God!</u>" — is only partially saved by the landscape of the concluding line. The octave recounts the circumstances of St. Bernard's statement and his theological quarrel with Gilbert de la Porrée at the Council of Rheims; the sestet laments the fact that Bernard's simple theology "fools / Misdefine", saints fail to preach, and churches ignore. Both before and after Bernard's time this theological simplicity was lost to mankind: "'Tis in the desert, now and heretofore". The introduction of a waste-land image in the final line refocuses the point of the sonnet and saves it from complete drabness of exposition.

Arnold's images do not make him a great sonneteer. In the

nineteenth century, Keats and Wordsworth were greater before him, and Rossetti, Meredith, Hopkins, and Bridges, after him. The point is that Arnold stamped memorable images of nature integrated throughout the poems. And this same device links his sonnets with his greatest poems: the sea in "Dover Beach", the Oxus stream in "Sohrab and Rustum", the Scholar Gipsy himself, the signal-elm in "Thyrsis", and the weeping children beside the walls of The Grande Chartreuse, "Forgotten in a forest-glade".

A second distinguishing feature of the Arnoldian sonnet is its classic simplicity and balance of phrase and line. The famous verse, "Who saw life steadily, and saw it whole", in "To a Friend" is an example. The simplicity lies in the choice of basically Anglo-Saxon words that contrast with the Latinized line that follows, "The mellow glory of the Attic stage". And the balance is achieved by the internal alliteration of s's in steadily and saw, bordered by the wh in Who and whole. Moreover, Arnold carefully introduces the verb saw in the third line of the octave, referring to Homer: "Saw The Wide Prospect, and the Asian Fen, / And Tmolus hill, and Smyrna bay, though blind". Homer's perception, according to Arnold, embraces Europe and Asia, but Sophocles, because of his "even-balanced soul" from "first youth" to "extreme old age", saw all of life —its inner motivations and its ultimate resignation. Homer is the wise "old man", but Sophocles is the "Singer of sweet Colonus, and its child" — the city of his birth and death. This simplicity and balance Arnold achieves by contrasting basic words saw, man, and child.

Classical balance of line and phrase, then, is illustrative of what Arnold tries to define in his two essays "On Translating Homer" and various other critical pieces like "The Study of Poetry". The key ideas are "simplicity", "severity", and "intense compression". In an otherwise undistinguished sonnet called "Religious Isolation", Arnold belabors as childish the concept that man should know or live by all the "holy secrets" of Nature. "Live by thy light, and earth will live by hers!" is the classic conclusion. Again the words are monosyllabic, the grammatical structure is the forceful imperative, and the only ornament is the emphatic alliteration of the l's. The tone contrasts with the long, somewhat Latinized words and involved structure of the first twelve lines. The conclusion is simple and severe, and compresses intensely the sonnet's main idea.

Occasionally Arnold creates this classic purposeful line by a

converse method in his use of polysyllabic, Latinized words
that stand out sharply from the surrounding monosyllabic flatness. In "Quiet Work" he begins:

One lesson, Nature, let me learn of thee,
One lesson which in every wind is blown,
One lesson of two duties kept at one.

Arnold then contrasts this simple Wordsworthian tone with the
explanation of the "One lesson":

Of toil unsevered from tranquillity —
Of labour, that in lasting fruit outgrows
Far noisier schemes, accomplished in repose,
Too great for haste, too high for rivalry!

The balanced alliteration of t's, l's, s's, and h's and the use of
Latinized words like unsevered, tranquillity, repose, and rivalry
(placed in key positions) all help to create the contrasting illusion
of classic grace. By taking advantage of English's contrasting
elements of Anglo-Saxon and Latin words, of alliteration and
rime, Arnold can achieve the grand style even in the small scope
of the sonnet.
   Indeed Arnold can occasionally capture the effect with surprising economy of image and language. In "Monica's Last Prayer"
he makes the reader aware of the austere grace of Monica's
Christian sentiment about burial:

                . . . lay me where I fall!
Everywhere heard will be the judgment-call;
But at God's altar, oh! remember me.

This starkly simple phraseology he juxtaposes beside the recollection of Monica's former selfish longing for "burial . . . by
the Libyan sea". The nature image, like the ending of "Sohrab
and Rustum" with the stars that "shine upon the Aral sea", is
beautiful but romantically false. The central idea of the opening
lines Arnold has made to seem honestly righteous when placed
beside the sight of a far-off Libyan sea and the rhetoric of "Yet
fervent had her longing been" for burial by the sea. If there is
an Arnoldian sonnet, its two clearest features are the integrated
image from nature and a skillful use of a balanced classic line.

Since Arnold was himself an editor and critic as well as a poet, the final word on the sonnet should come from him. Nowhere in all his prose criticism, however, does he comment significantly on the sonnet in general or on the sonnets of the major English poets. His attitude, therefore, can only be inferred. The great age of sonneteering, the Renaissance, Arnold did not admire. Of his favorite poet Milton, "master in the great style of the ancients", Arnold says almost nothing of the sonnets that obviously influenced his own. When he spoke at the dedication of the Childs' window in memory of Catherine Woodcock, Milton's secor wife, he refers to "Methought I saw my late espoused saint" only as "the famous sonnet". (38) In the essay "Thomas Gray" there is no mention of the well-known sonnet to Richard West that Wordsworth disliked, and in "John Keats" no sonnets are mentioned except as one may interpret "But in shorter things, where the matured power of moral interpretation, and the high archetechtonics which go with complete poetic development, are not required, he is perfect. The poems which follow prove it—prove it far better by themselves than anything which can be said about them will prove it. "(39) The selections from Keats, however, were not chosen by Arnold. The case with Wordsworth was different. When Arnold edited the selection from the works of that poet, he himself chose nine poems of "Ballad Form", thirteer "Narrative Poems", forty "Lyrical Poems", nine "Poems akin tc the Antique, and Odes", and sixty from Wordsworth's more than five hundred "Sonnets", because Arnold believed that Wordsworth "best work is in his shorter pieces". Arnold even confessed, "I can read with pleasure and edification <u>Peter Bell</u> and the whole series of Ecclesiastical Sonnets". (40)

Judging from Arnold's comments, one feels that he liked the sonnet as such well enough but somehow regretted that it was neither a "classic" nor a "modern" form. At least he did not dislike it as did Browning, nor did Arnold write such poor specimens as did Tennyson. In his most extended, if informal, comme on the sonnet Arnold takes the position of the "golden mean"— precisely as he himself practiced this verse: "The sonnet is an alluring form, but I doubt if it does not, when too much followed, disincline one for the others, which, after all, can do what it cannot do. On the other hand, in no form does the composer mar more clearly whether he is essentially poetical or prosaic. "(41)

As a young poet Arnold often used the sonnet as trial ground fo ideas that he developed further in some of his best poems. Later

97

as an Oxford professor and critic of literature and life he continued to write sonnets to prove to himself perhaps that he could
still turn a poetic line even "Though the Muse be gone away".
Viewed as a whole, Arnold's sonnets are the most memorable
among those of the first-generation Victorian poets, and no small
measure of their success is due to the variety of their subject
matter, to the metrical diversity of the early ones as contrasted
with the strict Petrarchan order of the later ones, and finally to
the Arnoldian quality of the integrated image and the classic line.
From the sequence of three about Rachel, to the pair to Republican Clough, to brief glimpses at personal living, to the great
issues of literature and philosophy Arnold saw the sonnet steadily
and whole.

NOTES

(1) Dougald B. MacEachen, "Tennyson and the Sonnet", VN, no.
14 (1958), p. 6. This is also the opinion of J.F.A. Pyre, The
Formation of Tennyson's Style (Madison: Univ. of Wisconsin
Press, 1921), and Paull F. Baum, Tennyson Sixty Years After
(Chapel Hill: Univ. of North Carolina Press, 1948).
(2) For a discussion of the number of Browning's sonnets, as
well as Tennyson's, see Chapters 2 and 3.
(3) The complement of twenty-nine is arrived at by including
"Sonnet to the Hungarian Nation" (Examiner, 1849) and "S.S.
'Lusitania'" (Nineteenth Century, 1879), neither of which Arnold
reprinted from their periodical publications.
(4) Kenneth Allott, ed., The Poems of Matthew Arnold (New York:
Barnes & Noble, 1965), lists 129 poems that Arnold published in
some form during his life (including "Aleric at Rome" and
"Cromwell", the Rugby and Newdigate prize poems), of which 29
are sonnets; the Library Edition (London, 1888), which Tinker
and Lowry call "the last which could have had the advantages of
the poet's arrangement", lists 115 poems, of which 27 are sonnets. I have used Allott's edition throughout this essay. Texts of
the sonnets occur there as follows:

98

(5) As has already been noted, "Sonnet" ("Two lessons, Nature, let me learn of thee") was placed first in The Strayed Reveller volume, and "Sonnet. To a Friend" ("Who prop, thou ask'st, in these bad days, my mind?") was probably placed between "Mycerinus" and "The Strayed Reveller" for contrastive purposes; the other nine were separately listed by their individual titles under Sonnets.
(6) The only important exception was in Poems (London, 1869) in two volumes - "Narrative and Elegiac" and "Dramatic and Lyric" - where the sonnets were split between the "Elegiac" and "Lyric" divisions.

(7) Arnold's introduction to his selection of Poems of Wordsworth (London, 1879) reprinted in Essays in Criticism, 2d ser. (London: Macmillan, 1896), p. 137.

(8) The exact dates of composition for all twenty-nine sonnets cannot be established with absolute accuracy, but most can be dated at least by month and year. The best sources for these dates are C.B. Tinker and H.F. Lowry, The Poetry of Matthew Arnold: A Commentary (London: Oxford Univ. Press, 1940), hereafter cited as Commentary, and The Poems of Matthew Arnold, ed. Kenneth Allott (New York: Barnes & Noble, 1965), hereafter cited as Allott, both of which use the letters, note-books, and Yale MSS as their primary sources.

(9) John Addington Symonds, to whom Arnold presented the Newdigate prize at Oxford, was fond of pointing to the great variety of sestets used among Renaissance poets. See, for example, his introduction to Animi Figura (London: Smith, Elder, 1882), pp. viii-ix, as a sensible antidote to much of the late Victorian fad for the "legitimate" theory of sonnet structure that grew up among critics like Theodore Watts-Dunton, Charles Tomlinson, Mark Pattison, and others.

(10) Letters of Matthew Arnold, ed. G.W.E. Russell (London: MacMillan, 1895), I, 208, hereafter cited as Letters.

(11) Commentary, p. 135. The entries in the printed Note-books, however, are not very revealing: e.g., "compose 2 sonnets" from the June 1863 "compose and read" list.

(12) Allott, p. 481.

(13) Matthew Arnold—poète: essai de biographie psychologique (Paris: M. Didier, 1947), p. 85.

(14) G.M. Young, Victorian England (New York: Doubleday, 1954), p. 42, n. 8.

(15) Letters, I, 232.

(16) See Allott, p. 488.

(17) Warren D. Anderson, Matthew Arnold and the Classical Tradition (Ann Arbor: Univ. of Michigan Press, 1965), p. 62.

(18) Matthew Arnold: The Poet as Humanist (Princeton: Princeton Univ. Press, 1967), pp. 221-22.

(19) A. Dwight Culler, Imaginative Reason: The Poetry of Matthew Arnold (New Haven, Conn.: Yale Univ. Press, 1966), p. 46.

(20) Commentary, p. 15, and Allott, p. 145. Both poems were called merely "Sonnets" in 1852, their present titles being added in 1853 and 1867, respectively.

(21) E. K. Brown, "Matthew Arnold and the Elizabethans", UTQ (1932) 351.

(22) "On the Modern Elements in Literature", Macmillan's Magazine, vol. 19 (1869), in Essays, Letters and Reviews by Matthew Arnold, ed. Fraser Neiman (Cambridge, Mass.: Harvard Univ. Press, 1960), pp. 8-10.

(23) Arnold: How to Know Him (Indianapolis, Ind.: Bobbs-Merrill, 1917), p. 163.

(24) UTQ 1 (1932): 343.

(25) The Note-books of Matthew Arnold, ed. H. F. Foster, Karl Young, and W. H. Dunn (London: Oxford Univ. Press, 1952), pp. 573, 576, 581.

(26) The Letters of Matthew Arnold to Arthur Hugh Clough, ed. H. F. Lowry (London: Oxford Univ. Press, 1932), p. 97.

(27) Stange, pp. 221-22. It seems to me that Professor Stange forgets Sonnets from the Portuguese when he says that "The conventions of the sonnet-cycle are radically different from those of the nineteenth-century love lyric", just as he seems unaware of the narrative tensions in Shakespeare's sonnets when he says that the sonneteer "sets out to praise his beloved as ingeniously as possible, to recount the joys and sufferings which his love has brought, and either to regret his inability to attain the beloved or to rejoice in having done so. " The point is that Mrs. Browning and Rossetti continue the generally held concept of the Elizabethan series, while Meredith, Symonds, and Blunt explore the pattern hinted in Shakespeare. Arnold's "Switzerland" and "Faded Leaves"—if they had been sonnet sequences—would fall in the latter group.

(28) "Instead of turning to God last night I wrote a sonnet, and poeticized till 10 o'clock. Composed 2 more in bed", Clough confided to his journal in 1835 (quoted in The Letters of Matthew Arnold to Arthur Hugh Clough, p. 8). In 1837 he published a little essay on "Sonnets in the Abstract" in The Rugby Magazine (quoted in Selected Prose Works of Arthur Hugh Clough, ed. Buckner B. Trawick [University: Univ. of Alabama Press, 1964 pp. 48-52). In 1844 Clough continued to be interested in the sonnet; in a letter to his friend Burbidge he wrote, "I have had but little holiday as yet myself, having been as thou well knowst, busily employed for a whole extra fortnight at Oxford in writing biographies and sonnets"; and unlike Arnold, who did not seem to care for Shakespeare's sonnets, Clough wrote again to Burbidge in the same year that he felt "fairly disposed to sub-

mit to" Charles Knight's theory of Shakespeare's sonnets (The Correspondence of Arthur Hugh Clough, ed. Frederick L. Mulhauser [Oxford: Clarendon Press, 1957], I, 131, 95).
(29) The Letters of Matthew Arnold to Arthur Clough, p. 104.
(30) Arnold the Poet (New York: Barnes & Noble, 1962), p. 57.
(31) Professor Allott gives no explanation of his strange statement that the "sight-rime" is "accidental" (Poems, p. 49).
(32) Culler, p. 34.
(33) Education and the University (London: Chatto & Windus, 1948), p. 75.
(34) Matthew Arnold, Modern English Writers' Series (Edinburgh: Blackwood, 1899), pp. 111-12.
(35) Ten Studies in the Poetry of Matthew Arnold (Durham, N.C.: Duke Univ. Press, 1958), p. 12. Baum summarizes much of the scholarship on this sonnet.
(36) See Theodore Morrison, "'Dover Beach' Revisited", Harper's 180 (1940) 235-44.
(37) William Sharp summarizes the point of view of Arnold's contemporaries in his "Notes" to Sonnets of This Century (London: Walter Scott, [1886]): "Familiar portions of the familiar work of one of the leading poets of our time, [the sonnets of Arnold] call for no special comments" (p. 273). Modern anthologists who include Arnold almost always include a sonnet or two.
(38) "Milton", Essays in Criticism, 2d ser. (London: Macmillan, 1896), pp. 59-60.
(39) Essays in Criticism, p. 120. The essay was originally prefixed to the selections from Keats in Ward's English Poets, vol 4 (1880).
(40) Arnold's introduction of his selections of Poems of Wordsworth (1879), reprinted in Essays in Criticism, 2d ser., (London: Macmillan, 1896), p. 161.
(41) Unpublished and undated letter to John Payne, cited in Commentary, p. 135.

5. THE MODERNITY OF MEREDITH'S MODERN LOVE

(A)

One can admire the sincerity of sentiment in Mrs. Browning's
Sonnets from the Portuguese, the convoluted beauty of Rossetti's
The House of Life and Bridges' The Growth of Love, and the
stark narrative of Blunt's Esther; but well after the passage of
a century it is only Meredith's Modern Love (1862) that still
seems completely relevant and enduring in both its form and
structure — its theme and organic artistry. One is almost tempt
to say that the poem must be reckoned first among the great son
net sequences of the nineteenth century. The most obvious de-
murral to this point of view, at least among purists, is the
question of the proper designation of the fifty sixteen-line sectio
that comprise the poem. Are they sonnets? And if they are not,
can Modern Love rightly be called a sonnet sequence?

Meredith himself called the stanzas sonnets. Writing in Janua
of 1862 to his good friend Captain Maxse, to whom the entire
volume was to be dedicated, he says, "I send you a portion of
proofs to the 'Tragedy of Modern Love'. There are wanting to
complete it 13 more sonnets."(1) Swinburne, himself a skilled
writer of sonnets, refers to the stanzas of Modern Love as "son
nets" — without qualification: in his well-known letter to the edit
of The Spectator (June 7, 1862) he uses the term three times an
avoids any synonym.

Twenty-three years later, replying to William Sharp, the edi
of Sonnets of This Century, Meredith says: "You are at liberty
make your use of the Sonnet you have named ["Lucifer in Starli¿
The Italians allow of 16 lines, under the title of 'Sonnets with a
Tail'. But the lines of 'Modern Love' were not designed for that
form."(2) Sharp, however, does not see Meredith's point, for
after quoting five of the "very remarkable sequence of sixteen-
line poems comprised under the heading Modern Love" in his
anthology, he labels them "essentially 'caudated sonnets'" as
opposed to "the single sonnet proper by Mr. Meredith which I
have given in my selection". (3) In his laconic reply Meredith
seems to be saying that his sonnets in Modern Love are not
traditional even in their expansion from fourteen to sixteen line
as an examination of their structure will confirm; but sonnets

they are — modern sonnets.

By the time Meredith came to write Modern Love he had considerable practice in composing single sonnets as well as groups
of sonnets. Among his early poems — "my boy's book in '51", as
he called it, (Letters, I, 124) — is a sonnet "John Lackland",
which was apparently part of a larger grouping, since in 1849 he
had sent to one of the editors of Chambers's Journal "some Sonnets on Two Kings of England, which may if you like form a
series. . . . I have a great many already finished".(4) And in
1853 he wrote to John W. Parker, publisher of his first volume
of poems, "I have other 'Pictures of the Rhine' but I thought six
enough" (Letters, I, 12). Both of these statements — even allow-
ing for youthful bragging in the quest of a publisher — attest
Meredith's earlier interest in the sonnet series before he planned
Modern Love. Judged by its working title "Kings of England" and
by the one extant sonnet "John Lackland", this series would seem
to echo Wordsworthian patterns of historical arrangement as
evidenced in Ecclesiastical Sonnets. In fact, at about this same
time, Meredith was trying his hand at a similar historical
approach in a group of quatrain poems about the English poets
from Chaucer to Wordsworth and to Keats. Certainly it is
Wordsworth who serves as model for the six "Pictures of the
Rhine", for the sonnets are "tour memorials" along the banks of
a river, partly recollected in tranquillity from Meredith's school
days at Neuwied on the Rhine and partly from his wedding trip
along that same river. Like Wordsworth's River Duddon, the
Rhine is seen at varying seasons, and the mutability of its legends
and landscapes is recorded.

In structure all eight of these early sonnets ("John Lackland",
the six Rhine sonnets, and "To Alex. Smith, the 'Glasgow Poet' ")
are fourteen lines in length and somewhat irregular in thought
division and rime pattern. Two characteristics stand out: a final
Alexandrine in six of the eight and a preference for the rime
pattern a b b a that is never extended beyond four lines. Before
1861, then, Meredith was demonstrably interested in the sonnet,
seeing it as a form for metrical experimentation in length of line
and pattern of rime; and he preferred his sonnets related to one
another in series.

When Meredith returned to poetry in the 1880's after a long
stretch of novel writing, he also returned to the sonnet. And like
Arnold, Meredith became a more conservative sonneteer. Of the
early sonnets not one of the eight follows either the Petrarchan

104

or Shakespearean rime pattern, while the thirty-eight written after the 1880's, like his famous "Lucifer in Starlight", tend to be Petrarchan in structure. And in "The Spirit of Shakespeare", "Camelus Saltat", "My Theme", and "The Teaching of the Nude" he continued to group sonnets—this time in pairs. (5)

Since Meredith wrote sonnets and groups of sonnets before and after _Modern Love_ and since he called the sections of the poem sonnets both before and long after he had written them, the poet must be given credit for knowing what he was about when he decided upon a verse form that he felt would be organically related to the subject he had in hand. For _Modern Love_ Meredith needed a verse form that would above all things be flexible: it should suggest the sonnet without being one in its strictest sense, its form evolving as the sonnet had once evolved—in the words of John Addington Symonds—"from the same germ as the Rispetto, Sesta Rima and Ottava Rima". (6) Instead of the Alexandrines used in "Pictures of the Rhine" to emphasize the separateness of each picture, Meredith seems in _Modern Love_ to wish to avoid the feeling of completion of each sonnet in this more narrative sequence. (7) By duplicating the use of the same quatrains of closed rime that he had used for the octaves of all his earlier sonnets, Meredith has hit upon a form that could suggest both the movement and countermovement of the Italian sonnet as well as the pointed summary or turn of comment of the Shakespearean pattern. In the first sonnet, for example, the two quatrains produce the effect of an Italian octave even though the rime scheme is a b b a c d d c.

I

By this he knew she wept with waking eyes:
That, at his hand's light quiver by her head,
The strange low sobs that shook their common bed
Were called into her with a sharp surprise,
And strangled mute, like little gaping snakes,
Dreadfully venonous to him. She lay
Stone-still, and the long darkness flowed away
With muffled pulses. Then, as midnight makes
Her giant heart of Memory and Tears
Drink the pale drug of silence, and so beat
Sleep's heavy measure, they from head to feet
Were moveless, looking through their dead black years,

By vain regret scrawled over the blank wall.
Like sculptured effigies they might be seen
Upon their marriage-tomb, the sword between;
Each wishing for the sword that severs all.

The break in the middle of the eighth line with the sentence beginning Then seems to signal the shift to the sestet: from the visual
reality of a bedroom to the imagined reality of the tomb. Yet
because the sestet is lengthened to eight and a half lines, the
sonnet movement flows beyond an end. The beginning of II, "It
ended, and the morrow brought the task", confirms the rushing
continuity. But the sonnets have not been reduced to stanzas:
though the pronoun It seems to point backwards, Sonnet II can be
read as a single understandable poem with It pointing forward to
its implied antithesis morrow and thereby an understood momen-
tous night as the antecedent. This same device opens Sonnet III:
"This was the woman; what now of the man?"—the referential
demonstrative pointing both backward and forward.

This sixteen-line sonnet serves equally well when Meredith
wishes to suggest the movement of a Shakespearean sonnet. In
XXX, for example, the poet-husband dissects the evolutionist's
idea of love: "What are we first? First, animals; and next / Intelligences at a leap; on whom / Pale lies the distant shadow of the
tomb". Those who understand the unity of intelligence and instinct
are "the scientific animals". (8) The last line of the poem is pre-
ceded by a dash: "Lady, this is my sonnet(9) to your eyes". The
effect is that of the Shakespearean couplet, but with a difference —
its brevity makes it more barbed and at the same time produces
an intellectual jolt rather than a rimed-couplet resolution.

With this flexible verse Meredith can ring changes on the two
basic types of sonnets as well as on variations and combinations
of the two. On the other hand, he can avoid the essential characteristics of sonnet movement in scenic and narrative sections and
achieve the effect of the connective prose links that the Italian
Renaissance poets sometimes used. Swinburne's favorite is an
example:

XLVII

We saw the swallows gathering in the sky,
And in the osier-isle we heard them noise.
We had not to look back on summer joys,

Or forward to a summer of bright dye:
But in the largeness of the evening earth
Our spirits grew as we went side by side.
The hour became her husband and my bride.
Love, that had robbed us so, thus blessed our dearth!
The pilgrims of the year waxed very loud
In multitudinous chatterings, as the flood
Full brown came from the West, and like pale blood
Expanded to the upper crimson cloud.
Love, that had robbed us of immortal things,
This little moment mercifully gave,
Where I have seen across the twilight wave
The swan sail with her young beneath her wings.

Yet with all these variations of structure the rime scheme —
a b b a c d d c e f f e g h h g — can remain fixed for the sake of
sustaining unity of form without the impeding artificiality of only
four or five rime sounds in the Petrarchan sonnet. Whatever one
may think of this pseudo-sonnet, it is unique — unique even in
Meredith's verse. He never used the form again, just as he never
wrote another poem in the style and spirit of Modern Love.
    One thing is certain: Meredith did not wish to continue the tradi-
tion of the verse style of the sonnet series of the Renaissance as
Mrs. Browning had done and as the parts of Rossetti's series
that he had been shown in manuscript seemed destined to do. Of
the Sonnets from the Portuguese there is no mention in Meredith's
letters, but of Aurora Leigh he writes, "I am glad Aurora Leigh
is so well received. I have not read it, but the extracts promise"
(Letters, I, 29). What interests Meredith in Mrs. Browning's
poetry is how she chooses to tell a modern semi-autobiographical
story in a verse novel, not in a Renaissance sonnet sequence. He
is apparently hopeful that the result will not be like what he was
to see a few years later in the laureate's Enoch Arden: "I'm a
little sick of Tennysonian green Tea. . . . I tell you that Enoch
Arden is ill done, and that in twenty years' time it will be de-
nounced as villainous weak, in spite of the fine (but too conscious)
verse. . . ." (Letters, I, 323). And he feels similarly about
Rossetti's projected sonnets. In 1861 he writes to Maxse that
Rossetti "is a poet, without doubt. He would please you more
than I do, or can, for he deals with essential poetry, and is not
wild, and bluff, and coarse; but rich, refined, royal-robed!"
(Letters, I, 121). The ironic implication in this comment is that

the friend to whom the volume is to be dedicated will probably not like it or understand the relationship of the form to the content any better than the average reader. For Maxse and this average reader Meredith placed a warning epigraph in the first edition of Modern Love:

This is not meat
For little people or for fools.

(B)

Just as the verse form of Modern Love is complicated in its evolution and precisely fitted for the unfolding of the tragically ironic "Love-Match"(10) that Meredith had in mind, so is the raw material complicated in its evolution. Though Meredith's early poetry usually finds its ideas for starting points in contemporary reality, like all good poets he re-creates to his immediate purpose.

Thus [he writes] my Jugglers, Beggars, etc., I have met on the road, and have idealized but slightly. I desire to strike the poetic spark out of absolute human clay. And in doing so I have the fancy that I do solid work—better than a carol in mid air. Note the 'Old Chartist', and the 'Patriot Engineer', that will also appear in Once a Week. They may not please you; but I think you will admit that they have a truth condensed in them. They are flints perhaps, and not flowers. Well, I think of publishing a volume of Poems in the beginning of '62, and I will bring as many flowers to it as I can (Letters, I, 110).

This letter indicates Meredith's frame of mind at about the time of the writing of Modern Love. And in writing of his own marital tragedy, he has enough perspective on himself and at the same time lacks enough perspective to give the poem a peculiar alertness of point of view. The seeming curious shifting between I and he allows Meredith to have both closeness and distance. An examination of the alternation between the first and third person reveals an alternation between the distanced calm of the third person and the immediate passion of the first person. And this was

precisely the tension from which Meredith wrote. His wife Mary
had left him in 1858, fleeing to the continent with Henry Wallis,
an artist on the fringe of the Pre-Raphaelite movement. The
years immediately following this event were crowded: The Ordeal
of Richard Feverel was published in 1859, Evan Harrington
appeared in Once a Week from February to October of 1860, and
in August of that same year Meredith succeeded John Forster as
reader for Chapman & Hall, having established a simple home
for himself and his little son Arthur at Copsham Cottage near
Esher in Surrey. (11) Consciously or unconsciously Meredith
was undoubtedly turning over in his mind his personal domestic
tragedy, preparing to use it as he had used his early experience
and those of his grandfather in Evan Harrington, and as he was
later to use his friend Maxse's life story in Beauchamp's Career.

Exactly when Modern Love was written is not easy to say.
Lionel Stevenson suggests "the winter months" of 1861. (12) The
scant evidence of the letters would seem to bear this date out.
But it need not necessarily be assumed that Meredith began the
poem only after his wife's death in October of 1861. It may well
be that the poem was started as early as 1859 and that Meredith
planned to end it with the flight of his wife to the continent, as
the Meynells and Sydney Cockerell believed. (13) Meredith certainly departed from the general outline of the biographical "facts" in
the concluding sections of the poem.

Almost all critics agree, however, that the main situation of
Modern Love centers in Meredith's own ill-fated first marriage.
William Meredith's comment in his edition of his father's letters
is typical:

> Two highly strung temperaments — man and wife — each
> imaginative, emotional, quick to anger, cuttingly satirical
> in dispute, each an incomparable wielder of the rapier of
> ridicule, could not find domestic content within the narrow
> bounds of poverty and lodgings. (14)

With the possible exception of the word poverty this sentence
might well serve as a statement of the situation in Modern Love
itself.

Critics are often warned that they should avoid the biographic
fallacy. But with Meredith, says V. S. Pritchett, "we are faced
with the biographical necessity if we are to get to the heart of
his very intensive manner". (15) Early critics like Hammerton

and Priestly comment with considerable restraint about the
biographical material in Modern Love. Later critics like
Gordon George, Siegreid Sassoon, and Lionel Stevenson discuss
the relationship between certain of the actual biographical situ-
ations and the poetic re-creations. (16) All agree that the struggle
between the two antagonists — the I-and-he and Madam — are
emotionally based on Meredith himself and his wife. Madam's
lover plays a minor and almost off-stage role in the poem, and
strangely enough even the biographers say little about him. His
most famous picture "The Death of Chatterton" in the Tate
Gallery hints something of the story. Meredith is without doubt
the model for Chatterton. Knowing Meredith's interest in illus-
trations for his poems and his friendship with Rossetti, Millais,
and other Pre-Raphaelites, one hardly escapes the feeling that
Meredith knew, perhaps entertained, and certainly sat for
Henry Wallis, at least for this remarkable Pre-Raphaelite study
of the eighteenth-century poet. (17) None of the biographers or
critics, however, is entirely helpful in identifying the biographical and sublimated affair with "My Lady". Gordon George
baldly states in the midst of his chapter on Evan Harrington:
"For five years she [Janet Duff Gordon] was, next to Arthur,
the person who meant most to him, and with whom he associated
his choicest words of praise and passion. None other than she
can be the 'lady' of Modern Love" (p. 109). Stevenson takes the
opposite point of view: "Meredith probably invented the episode
[with the 'lady'] to give symmetry to the situation and also to
make it typical of the artificial social complexities he intended
to impugn" (p. 104). Neither of these statements is entirely
accurate.

The "Lady" of the sequence is sketched with more fullness
than is Madam's lover, who according to the husband's wrath
"shall be crushed until he cannot feel . . . If he comes beneath
a heel". (18) She is introduced in Sonnet XIV as "a gold-haired
lady". Throughout the poem this feature is her most often-
mentioned physical attribute; in Sonnet XXXIX she is the poet's
"golden crownéd rose". Besides a character of "large browed
steadfastness" she has those rare gifts of beauty, common
sense, and wit. If Janet Duff Gordon is "My Lady" of the poem,
as Gordon George maintains, (19) even a cursory glance at the
dates of the chief events of Meredith's life from 1849 to 1862
reveals the fact that insofar as the biographical significance of
the poem is concerned something is awry.

After their marriage in 1849 and a sojourn on the continent, the Merediths settled at the Limes, a boarding-house at Weybridge. Here they came to know the wealthy and socially prominent Duff Gordons, who with their attractive children frequently held open house for the intellectuals of the neighborhood. To little Janet and his own stepdaughter Meredith delighted to read passages from the Arabian Nights tale, The Shaving of Shagpat, which he was writing about that time. In 1853, however, the Merediths moved across the Thames to live with Mary's father, the recently widowed Thomas Love Peacock of Shelleyan fame. And there in June, 1853, their son Arthur Gryffydh was born. By this move the Merediths apparently lost contact with the Duff Gordons.

It was not until 1859, after his marriage debacle and subsequent dissatisfaction with London lodgings, that Meredith moved to rural Surrey and again saw Janet, now a young lady just past sixteen. (20) She was riding one morning to the Esher station when a small boy stumbled and fell in front of her horse. When she took the child home to his father, she was recognized at once. "Oh! my Janet! Don't you know me? I am your Poet!" (21) exclaimed Meredith. There is little doubt that Janet meant a great deal to the young writer at a very bleak period in his life. Of this time Mrs. Ross wrote later: "We used to take long walks together. . . . My poet would recite poetry or talk about his novels. I made him write down some of the verses he improvised as we sat among the heather. . . ."(22) And in a manuscript version of Sonnet XXXII of Modern Love it is quite clear that Meredith did not mean originally for the affair with the Lady to even seem Platonic. The published version reads:

To see her lie
With her fair visage an inverted sky
Bloom-covered. . . .

In the "unrevised . . . MS., Meredith bluntly wrote, 'To see her lie . . . Beneath me' ".(23) Though Meredith appeared chagrined at the marriage of this charming young daughter of Sir Alexander and Lady Duff Gordon to a man even older than himself in December, 1860, he realized that marriage for him and Janet was scarcely possible. Mary Meredith was back in England living alone, and "after ten years in the [writing] profession [Meredith] could barely afford a lonely cottage to house himself and his little boy". (24) His love for Janet, therefore, was sublimated into the prose and poetry of the moment.

There was almost a generation that separated the real models for the Lady and Madam in Modern Love. In actual life they could never have known each other as adults, and the dramatic meeting between the two, when they compliment one another on their physical defects, could never have taken place, for Mary Meredith fled to the continent with Wallis in 1858 after having spent time the year before with him in Wales. Though she returned to England in 1859, she died in 1861 without ever seeing Meredith again. The poet-husband in Modern Love could never have written love letters to "My Lady" in his wife's presence, nor is it likely that the Lady would have appealed to him to return to his wife. In short, Mary Meredith never knew Janet Duff Gordon except as a child of nine or ten years.

From this illustration it is evident that the raw material and its re-created use in Modern Love is far from simple. As a literary achievement the poem does not stand or fall by a criterion of biographical truth. Whether it is an autobiographical account or a weaving of halftruths and psychological rationalisations is not a matter of artistic importance. But the reader and critic who search for personal history in the poem must always be aware that art has not obeyed chronological fact.

It is, therefore, a critical error to conceive of Modern Love as a narrative sequence of Meredith's marriage debacle: its causes and results. Those stanzas which portray the intimacies of husband and wife and their bitter, silencing hatred for one another may well be autobiographical. There is little reason to believe otherwise. The so-called "philandering episode" (Sonnets XXVII-XL) may mirror the poet's infatuation for the charming Janet whom Meredith had already made the Rose Jocelyn of Evan Harrington—there is an obvious connection between the name Rose of the novel and the "golden crownëd rose" of the poem. But juxtaposing these two episodes into a single tragedy is not "according to history", just as the ending of the poem also departs from facts, for there was really no discovering of Mary Meredith wandering by the seashore, no midnight poisoning-suicide in her husband's presence, no momentary reconciliation of peace when they "saw the swallows gathering in the sky".

Just as Meredith used his own experiences over and over again in his novels, so in Modern Love does he weave his tragic

marriage venture with Mary Ellen Nicolls and his pleasant friendship with Janet Duff Gordon into a bitter, dramatic sequence, the
incidents of which are partly true and partly fictional, rearranged
in time and place, and peopled like the novels with characters
drawn chiefly from real life. (25)

(C)

The complicated duality of the verse form — a sonnet sequence
composed of seizains that suggest various types of sonnets — as
well as subtle subject matter — autobiography re-arranged in
time, place, and resolution — point the way to the characteristics
that make Modern Love a great timeless modern poem. One of
the characteristics studied with thoroughness by recent scholars
is the matter of the unification of the images. Norman Friedman
discovers a dominance of "image clusters": the wife, for
example, is represented by snake-venom-poison images while
the disillusionment of the husband is seen in terms of murder-
knife-wound-blood images. Elizabeth Cox Wright makes the
point that almost every word of the first sonnet "is significant
in later stanzas as a repeated image or part of a repeated image"
Norman Kelvin finds that war images dominate and unify the
poem: the "sword that severs all", the "warrior horse", the
"fatal knife". John Henry Smith believes that animal images tend
to become evident as Meredith works out man's animal sensu-
ality and hypocrisy in the natural world. (26)
     Whatever the contradictions and repetitions in these recent
essays, they attest the importance twentieth-century readers
have found in the message and meaning of imagery, a revelation
that escaped most of the Victorian readers of the poem who were
used to Tennyson's moral ordering and Arnold's explicit as-
sertions. The imagery is undoubtedly a part of Meredith's tragic-
comic method of attacking established patterns long inherent in
the sonnet series. Mrs. Browning applies the feminine bias, and
Rossetti elaborates the traditional. But for Meredith there are
no Eros-Cupids (Greek or Ovidian) in Arcadia or Willowwood,
no elaborate conceits about the Heart, and no stereotyped Sonnet
Lady. Meredith's dapper Cupid is merely a wiley hairdresser
(VII); the husband can be a "much-adored delightful Fairy Prince"
visually recognizable by "hindward feather and . . . forward toe'
only at the unforgivable expense of being willing "to mince / The

facts of life" (X). And when "My Lady" makes her appearance, even though she is traditionally blonde and golden haired, she has wit (brain) as well as vivacity (blood) and charm (spirit); she is neither entirely cruel nor entirely untouchably amorous (XXXI, XXXII).

This spirit of working—with a difference—within the sonnet tradition makes <u>Modern Love</u> seem both timeless and modern. The point of view, which most commentators take pains to explicate as if Meredith ineptly shifts <u>he</u> and <u>I</u>, is still another example of broadening the genre. When the poet-husband speaks of himself as <u>he</u>, he lends omniscient distance to the narrative element. When he uses the <u>I</u>, the immediacy of the first-person rushes in. This method is peculiarly effective in the sonnet sequence with its blend of action, implied action, and lyric meditation, as well as its separateness of stanzas and its unity of the whole. As a novelist Meredith was aware of the virtues of different ways of conveying a story and of involving the reader in that story. And like Meredith's admirer, Henry James, who evolved a kind of central intelligence that operates with the effect of both the first- and third-person, Meredith employs the shocking shifts that he cannot use effectively in prose stories. In Sonnet III this device is carefully introduced. By giving "the man", the wife's lover, no name because he is ineffable not in virtue but in baseness, the narrator must suddenly shift to the first-person for pronominal reference to himself: "Lord God, who mad'st the thing so fair, / See that I am drawn to her even now!" This simple beginning Meredith pursues with increasing subtlety. Occasionally <u>I</u> ironically and parenthetically speaks asides (VII, lines 3-4); more often the overpowering emotions called forth by the momentary situation force the distance to crumble and the <u>I</u> to break through (X). In the first section of the poem, the bitter estrangement of husband and wife (I-XXV), the point of view is dominated by the uneasy restraint of the omniscient third-person while in the second section, the attempt of the husband to find solace with his Lady (XXVII-XL), the <u>I</u>'s tend to dominate. In the final ten sonnets the <u>I</u>'s and <u>she</u>'s alternate with <u>we</u>'s until the return to the omniscience of the final two sonnets, parallel to the first two.

Another way to see this shifting point of view is in terms of "the divided self". Discussing Rossetti's <u>The House of Life</u>, Professor Miyoshi believes that Rossetti attempts to achieve a "Dantean fusion of spirit and flesh, heaven and earth. . . .

114

Finally in 'He and I' (XCIII), the speaker is so hounded by his
other self that he no longer knows which of the two is living his
life. "(27) Although Miyoshi does not examine Modern Love in
the context of his thesis, he well might have done so. Meredith,
who had read many of Rossetti's sonnets in manuscript, aimed
in an opposite direction as he also did in matters of style: I is
the impulsive, romantic animal, he represents the rational,
tragic compromise. And the two forces interact dramatically
to form the blood, brain, and spirit of Meredith's later ideal
triad of the human animal.

Just as the point of view is an artistic contradiction of older
techniques, the blend of the lyric and narrative within the tradition of the sonnet sequence makes Modern Love the most
seminal poem in its genre since Shakespeare's Sonnets. C. S.
Lewis insists that after Petrarch abandoned the practice of prose
links between sonnet groupings which Dante and others had used,
the sonnet sequence should not be considered "a way of telling a
story. . . . It is a form which exists for the sake of prolonged
lyrical meditation. "(28) The trouble with this generalization is
that few people can read Shakespeare's Sonnets without feeling
that a story lurks in the background—and not the usual one of
the prostrate lover and the cruel mistress. Indeed, the "story"
has been so variously interpreted that for many readers the
cryptic puzzle all but overshadows the lyric power of the individual sonnets. Shakespeare or his printer wittingly or unwittingl
opened the door onto a new view of a lyric medium. Milton, on
the other hand, seemed to wish to free the sonnet from the shackl
of some of its Renaissance conventions by broadening its subject
matter and placing the emphasis squarely on the single sonnet in
preference to a series. The major poets of the eighteenth century
neglected the sonnet altogether. By the end of the century the
Wartons and Bowles had inspired Wordsworth and Coleridge to
restore the tradition of the series, using politics, the natural
world, and personal philosophy for subject matter. Mrs. Brownir
and Dante and Christina Rossetti proved the sonnet sequence a
still viable mode for meditations about love. Among the Victorian
poets, however, it is Meredith who pushes the genre in its new
direction without destroying its indirect lyric quality. To view
Modern Love, therefore, as entirely made up of fifty chapters of
a "naked novel" or entirely as a gallery of "Rembrandt etchings"
is unwise. It is neither; rather it is both.

So powerful is the hinted narrative of Shakespeare's Sonnets that it was inevitable that the English sonnet sequence would sooner or later develop in this direction. Wordsworth avoids the narrative approach except in the journey pattern and Mrs. Browning records the relatively simple design of a courtship that moves from quiet doubt to happy culmination. Meredith, on the other hand, tells a psychologically complicated story with four characters that begins in medias res, employs occasional flashbacks to happier days, dramatizes certain scenes, and unfolds the internalized thoughts of the narrator.

After the husband and wife

. . . have ceased to love. . . they attempt to keep alive what is dead. The wife has an admirer, and the husband, in turn, seeks distraction in another woman. All are playing at cross purposes; all are in a tangle of nerves and sentimentalities. Finally the wife flees — to leave the husband free to the other. He follows her and brings her home with him, but that night she calls him to her bed, kisses him, and dies of her own hand. (29)

Such is a typical summary of the action of Modern Love. Yet inescapable is the fact that one half of the summary is drawn from Sonnets I, II, XLVII, and XLIX. To mark a sharp distinction among narration, implied narration, and various forms of lyric meditation is not a simple task, especially not for Modern Love where the skill of the poem lies in the inweaving. But when one starts with a conventional premise that the action, at least in a scenic sense, usually occurs at a particular time in a particular place, he can make an interesting discovery about the structure of Modern Love. Almost half of the sonnets are developed in a scenic sense: the dramatic action takes place before the eyes of the reader. (30)

The first sonnet, for example, takes place at midnight in the bedroom of the husband and wife, both of whom wakefully feign sleep. Since II, III, and IV are lyric meditations against this background, the end of I introduces a time–death simile that bridges toward the rationalizations that follow:

Like sculptured effigies they might be seen
Upon their marriage–tomb, the sword between;
Each wishing for the sword that severs all.

Within the meditations that extend over the next three sonnets
cerebral action is also apparent:

>   Lord God, who mad'st the thing so fair,
> See that I am drawn to her even now!
> It cannot be such harm on her cool brow
> To put a kiss? (III)

Though elements of action and assertion are intertwined, the
general pattern is clear enough. In Sonnet V time and place are
sharply restored: "Familiar was her shoulder in the glass, /
Through that dark rain". On a rainy day in his wife's dressing
alcove "A message from her set his brain aflame". In Sonnet VI
the images of I, II, and III—midnight sobs, Love's ghost, tears,
lips and forehead—all meet in seeming agony; but

> —Beneath the surface this while by the fire
> They sat, she laughing at a quiet joke.

Occasionally the scene is fully drawn and sustained: XVI recalls
their days of courtship before the fire in "Our library-bower";
XXIV is at a Christmas "country house"; XVII is a dinner party,
where the guests see the "golden . . . marriage-knot" that is in
reality "Love's corpse-light shine". A few scenes are even sustained in dramatic narration over several sonnets: XXXVII-XL
reveal an evening dinner on "the garden terrace". The four
sonnets are linked by figures and images and by the husband's
thinking and speaking, and the silver laughter of Meredith's
comedy hangs over the approaching tragedy. And Sonnets XLI
and XLII form another midnight bedroom scene.
   There are even a few discursive dramatic interludes for contrast like XVIII, which draws the sort of rural scene that Hardy
was later to make famous: Jack and Tom are "paired with Moll
and Meg". They do not play at subtleties: "They have the secret
of the bull and lamb", though its source may be the same as the
later Shropshire lad denotes—beer. Sonnet XXXIII recalls a
Raphael picture in the Louvre and links it to a letter to "My
Lady" that Madam may read as he writes, just as he read one
of her letters to "the man" in Sonnet XV—this sort of juxtaposition makes the action and the meditation continually dramatic.
Even in essentially meditative sonnets the devices of dramatic
narration are employed. Professor Friedman put this matter

well: "On several occasions [the husband] apparently speaks directly to Madam or his Lady (e.g., XI, XIV, XXIV, XXVII, XXVIII), but even there he seems to be doing so only in his mind. . . . In consequence, the reader must guess at the line of the action in terms of the husband's response to it. "(31) And in similar fashion the sonnets of discursive interludes become psychologically dramatic as they reveal the husband's mind.

The blurring of the lines between lyric and narrative is the dominant feature of Modern Love —a feat that becomes all the more admirable the closer the examination. In fact, Modern Love joins in this respect the Victorians' search for the outer extent to genres: Browning's The Ring and the Book is a long novel, Swinburne's sonnet sequence in Act I, scene 2 of Locrine is strict drama, Blunt's Natalia's Resurrection, though in the form of a sonnet sequence, is in reality a short story, and Pater's Renaissance essays and Imaginary Portraits are often lyric poems. With this principle in view the total concept of Modern Love becomes clearer. The pseudo-sonnet of sixteen lines at first puzzling becomes satisfying as it suggests the modes and varieties of sonnet types while keeping its own form fixed. The shifting point of view at first disturbing becomes one of the dramatic means by which the narrative moves forward and the character of the husband is revealed. To be aware of the lyric-narrative interweaving is to perceive the abnormal normality of a new mode. Push this mode too far in either direction: on the one hand it returns like a stretched rubber band to the tradition of Petrarch, Sydney, Rossetti, and Bridges; on the other hand, the sonnet may become a mere stanza in a long narrative poem like Symonds' Stella Maris. Without Modern Love there may well have been no latter-day developmental sequences like those of William Ellery Leonard, W.H. Auden, and John Berryman.

In the intermingling of genre characteristics Modern Love achieves its modernity. The bitter edge of the word Modern in its title may by now not seem quite so ironic as it seemed in 1862, but without doubt the poem is "an early chapter in that history of the liberation of sexual relations from summary and conventional judgment that has been going on from Meredith's day to our own". (32) In his subject matter Meredith succeeds by keen insights and honest analysis. There is no moralizing conclusion to the poem:

Passions spin the plot:

We are betrayed by what is false within. . . . (XLII)
Ah, what a dusty answer gets the soul
When hot for certainties in this our life! (L)

In dealing with a contemporary subject Meredith succeeds where
Tennyson, Clough, Mrs. Browning, and Patmore largely fail.
So well does he succeed that after a century the judgment of
Arthur Symonds still stands both for the content and the structure
of the poem: ". . . among the masterpieces of contemporary
poetry Modern Love is the most distinctly modern poem ever
written. There has been nothing like it in English poetry. "(33)

NOTES

(1) The Letters of George Meredith, ed. C. L. Cline (Oxford:
Clarendon Press, 1970), I, 128 (hereafter cited in the text as
Letters).
(2) Elizabeth A. Sharp, William Sharp (Fiona Macleod): A
Memoir (New York: Duffield, 1910), p. 114. (These three
sentences constitute the entire letter, which is reprinted in
Letters, II, 798.)
(3) Sonnets of This [Nineteenth] Century (London: Walter Scott,
[1886]), pp. 307-310.
(4) Letters, I, 7-8. (These sonnets were not published by
Chambers's and, except for "John Lackland", are not known to
be extant, if they ever existed.)
(5) The Poetical Works of George Meredith, with Some Notes
by G. M. Trevelyan (New York: Scribner's, 1912) lists 48 sonnets (exclusive of Modern Love): 8 written in the 1850's, 2 in
the 1860's and 38 after 1880. All citations to the poetry are
from this text.
(6) Letter from Symonds to William Sharp in Memoir, p. 119.
Symonds discusses this matter of the origin of the sonnet more
fully in his Renaissance in Italy (I, 264ff) and Sharp in his
Sonnets of This Century (pp. xxiiff). While Meredith was not
an Italian scholar, he was a thorough philosophical "evolutionist"—as he had expounded humorously in "By the Rosanna" and
seriously in "Ode to the Spirit of Earth in Autumn", both written
at about the same time as Modern Love.
(7) This is the point of Willie D. Reader, "Stanza Form in
Meredith's Modern Love", VN, No. 38 (Fall, 1970), pp. 26-27,

though the author does not consider Modern Love in relation to Meredith's other sequences.

(8) Meredith's own prose explanation of this sonnet to Maxse, who evidently is puzzled by Nature's speech, can be found in one of the interesting new letters in Cline's edition of Letters, I, 128.

(9) Meredith's use of the word sonnet is interesting here: it ironically harks back to the loose Elizabethan sense of "love lyric", and because it is "my sonnet" of sixteen lines it emphasizes the modernity of the present variation of "legitimate" sonnets.

(10) Meredith's working title for Modern Love (Letters, I, 116).

(11) Lionel Stevenson, The Ordeal of George Meredith: A Biography (New York: Scribner's, 1953), pp. 69, 78-79.

(12) Stevenson, The Ordeal of George Meredith, p. 103.

(13) Meredith "expounded" the poem to Mrs. Meynell. See Wilfrid Scawen Blunt, My Diaries (New York: Knopf, 1922), II, 120-121. The late poet laureate, C. Day Lewis, who is a careful student of Meredith, also argues for an earlier date: ". . . my own conjecture is that its basic theme had been contemplated, many of its key images formed, and perhaps a few detached sonnets written before this [Mary Meredith's death]" (see his edition of Modern Love [London: Rupert Hart-Davis, 1948], p. xvii).

(14) The Letters of George Meredith: Collected and Edited by His Son (London: Scribner's, 1912), I, 5.

(15) George Meredith and English Comedy (New York: Random House, 1969), p. 33.

(16) J.A. Hammerton, George Meredith: His Life and Art in Anecdote and Criticism (London: Grant Richards, 1909), pp. 7ff; J.B. Priestley, George Meredith, Engl. Men of Letters Ser. (New York: Macmillan, 1926), pp. 17ff; R.E. Sencourt [R.E. George Gordon], The Life of George Meredith (New York: Scribner's, 1929), pp. 60ff; Siegfried Sassoon, Meredith (New York: Viking, 1948) pp. 47ff; Stevenson, The Ordeal of George Meredith, pp. 103ff.

(17) There is no "official" or definitive biography of Meredith; of those that now exist Lionel Stevenson's is the best. The greatest detail about Wallis, however, is to be found in Jack Lindsay, George Meredith: His Life and Work (London: Bodley Head, 1956). Without disclosing his source Lindsay states: "The Chatterton picture was done in the Gray's Inn Chambers

of Austin Daniel of <u>The Monthly Observer</u>" (p. 82).
(18) The first edition of the poem reads "our heel".
(19) Meredith's letters and Janet Ross's biography, <u>The Fourth Generation</u> (London: Constable, 1912) bear out part of this contention.
(20) <u>Who's Who</u> (1926) gives her birth as 1842.
(21) Ross, p. 48.
(22) Ross, p. 50.
(23) Phyllis Bartlett, "A Manuscript of Meredith's 'Modern Love' <u>The Yale University Library Gazette</u>, 40 (1966), 187.
(24) Stevenson, p. 81.
(25) For an earlier discussion of the Lady see my "A Note on 'My Lady' of <u>Modern Love</u>", <u>MLQ</u>, 7 (1946), 311-314.
(26) The following works are in the order mentioned in this paragraph: "The Jangled Harp: Symbolic Structure in 'Modern Love'" <u>MLQ</u>, 18 (1957), 9-26; "The Significance of the Image Pattern in Meredith's <u>Modern Love</u>", <u>VN</u>, No. 13 (1958), 1-9; <u>A Troubled Eden: Nature and Society in the Works of George Meredith</u> (Stanford: Univ. Press, 1961), 25-35; <u>Hiding the Skeleton: Imager in Feverel and Modern Love</u> (Lincoln, Nebr.: Nebraska Wesleyan Univ. Press, 1966), 65-69.
(27) Masao Miyoshi, <u>The Divided Self: A Perspective on the Literature of the Victorians</u> (New York: New York Univ. Press, 1969), pp. 256, 258.
(28) <u>English Literature in the Sixteenth Century</u> (Oxford: Clarendc Press, 1954), p. 327.
(29) William Chislett, <u>George Meredith: A Study and Appraisal</u> (Boston: R. G. Badger, 1925), p. 179.
(30) The following sonnets are for the most part "narrative": I, V, VI, XV, XVI, XVII, XXI, XXIII, XXXIII, XXXV, XXXVI, XXXVII, XXXIX, XLI, XLII, XLIII, XLV, XLVI, XLVII, XLVIII, XLIX.
(31) "The Jangled Harp", p. 12. The fascination of this problem is underlined by the fact that Professor Friedman classifies Sonnet XXVII as meditative while I list it as narrative in the main
(32) Graham Hough, ed., <u>Selected Poems of George Meredith</u> (London: Oxford Univ. Press, 1962), p. 7.
(33) "Sir William Watson", <u>Forum</u> 67 (1922), 486.

6. JOHN ADDINGTON SYMONDS: THE END OF A CENTURY

(A)

John Addington Symonds (1840-1893) was a man of many interests.
As the biographer of Boccaccio and Michelangelo; as the translator of the autobiography of Cellini, the sonnets of Campanella
and Michelangelo, and the memoirs of Count Gozzi; as the author
of studies of Dante, Sidney, Jonson, Shelley, and Whitman; as
philosophical critic of the Greek poets and Shakespeare's predecessors in the English drama, and as a writer of travel books
about Greece, Italy, and Switzerland, Symonds was well known
to scholars and to general readers of the late nineteenth century.
Although to twentieth-century students these works now seem
somewhat superficial and dated, Symonds' seven-volume work
Renaissance in Italy has stood the test of time and has become
a popular classic by a patient vulgariseur, as Symonds called
himself. His voluminous correspondence has recently been
edited in three volumes, (1) but the autobiography that he labored
over with much care in his last years—the outgrowth of his
somewhat abortive collaboration with Havelock Ellis in Sexual
Inversion—remains to be published after 1976. (2)
   The availability of the autobiography and the complete correspondence, along with his twenty-five or so published works,
will doubtless herald within the next decade a complete revalu-
ation of John Addington Symonds. It may well be that scholar,
critic, biographer, translator, and poet will come off second
best and that Symonds the chronicler of himself and his times—
the "woeful Victorian" of the title of the American edition of
Mrs. Grosskurth's recent biography—will emerge as the memorable Symonds. To remain a respected pater-familias, a
scholarly lecturer and writer, the friend of men as different as
Benjamin Jowett and Robert Louis Stevenson, and at the same
time defend idealistically a belief in and practice of homosexuality, was no mean feat for Symonds or for his Victorian
world—public or private. But it was a poet above all things
that Symonds most longed to be. Since this aspect of his career
has been long overshadowed by Symonds the critic-historian and
most recently by Symonds the man, it is now time to look again
at Symonds the poet, especially the sonneteer.

In childhood young Johnnie had played with his sisters at bouts-rimés, as the young Rossettis did in their family circle. At Harrow Symonds took long walks with the Rev. John Smith during which they recited alternate passages from Shelley, Keats, and Tennyson. (3) In these poetic interests he was encouraged by his physician father, a man of learning and culture with a passion for all the arts and sciences. At Oxford Symonds pursued his love of poetry. He again took long walks, at times following the route of Arnold's Scholar-Gipsy. And it was Matthew Arnold himself who in the summer term of 1860 presented Symonds the Newdigate Prize for his poem on the Escorial:

> When I came to recite my poem in the rostrum, Matthew
> Arnold, then our Professor of Poetry, informed me very
> kindly, and in the spirit of sound criticism, that he had
> voted for me, not because of my stylistic qualities, but
> because I intellectually grasped the subject, and used its
> motives better and more rationally than my competitors. (4)

Late in his life when Symonds wrote this passage in his auto-biography, he had come to accept in part Arnold's prophetic judgment. Earlier, however, he resented the fact that friends and reviewers never found his poetry as good as his prose. When Mrs. Clough, whose husband's verse he helped edit, told him that his own poetry was scarcely worth pursuing, Symonds loftily informed her that he could not give up the struggle just because God "has made me only a potential & not a real poet. I shall never cease writing poetry. It is the only thing I like. I hate the development of thought in prose. "(5) In his most prolific period Symonds published four volumes of verse in rapid succession: Many Moods (1878), New and Old (1880), Animi Figura (1882), and Vagabunduli Libellus (1884). In addition to translating several Italian poets, Symonds also issued Wine, Women and Song (1884), his version of the drinking songs and love lyrics of wandering medieval students. (6) And in 1880 when he closed his Bristol home, Clifton Hill House, in preparation for building a new one at Davos Platz in Switzerland, Symonds confessed to burning "oceans of verses". (7)

The sonnet is Symonds' favorite verse form. In fact, Animi Figura and Vagabunduli Libellus are composed entirely of sonnets. Depending upon the method of counting slightly altered versions of the same poem, Symonds published some 340 son-

nets. This figure places him among the most prolific sonneteers
during the sonnet's most prolific period—among the company of
Isaac Williams, Charles Tennyson Turner, Aubrey de Vere, and
Wilfrid Scawen Blunt, all of whom published well over three
hundred sonnets. Furthermore, most of Symonds' sonnets are
intended as parts of sequences rather than as separate poems.
Aside from the dedicatory sonnet to Horatio Brown, Animi
Figura's 140 sonnets contain only three that are not grouped with
at least one other sonnet. "The Thought of Death", on the other
hand, contains 22, and "Stella Maris" in the more miscellaneous
Vagabunduli Libellus has 67.

It is with this aspect of his sonnets—his theories of grouping—
that Symonds made his most significant contribution to the genre.
The quality of his sonnets as poems is not of a high order, and it
is well, at the outset, to consider briefly this fact. Like much of
his other poetry there is a certain flat tone to his sonnets: he
uses too many words, too many adjectives, and too facilely strings
them together. Van Wyck Brooks selects the fifth sonnet of "Intellectual Isolation" as "most characteristic" of Symonds' sonneteering:(8)

It is the center of the soul that ails:
   We carry with us our own heart's disease
   And craving the impossible, we freeze
The lively rills of love that never fails.
What faith, what hope will lend the spirit sails
   To waft her with a light spray-scattering breeze
   From the Calypso isle of Phantasies,
Self-taught, self-gendered, where the daylight pales?

Where wandering visions of foregone desires
   Pursue her sleepless on a stony strand;
   Instead of stars the bleak and baleful fires
Of vexed imagination, quivering spires
   That have nor rest nor substance, light the land
   Paced by lean hungry men, a ghostly band.

This is a proper enough sonnet, somewhat reminiscent of
Shakespeare and Swinburne, but nowhere does it take fire.

Even though Symonds' poetry leaves much to be desired as
poetry, his individual sonnets are structurally interesting. As a
student of Italian literature he was well aware of the development

and practice of sonnet writing, particularly among the Renaissanc
poets. He follows in his own sonnets the basic principles of the
Italian poets: an octave that rimes abba abba; a sestet that varies
with the needs of the poem. Symonds rarely attempts to keep the
same rime pattern for sestets of sonnets in sequence lest an artificiality and monotony mark the poem. But by far the most interes
ing features in Symonds' work in the sonnet form are his various
methods of linking sonnets and his theoretical comments upon his
intentions.

Animi Figura, a group of 140 meditative sonnets, is in the main
the work of Symonds' first years in Switzerland, as he attempted
to arrest his tuberculosis. Confined to his hammock, he passed
the late summer days of 1877 listening to his wife read Boswell's
Johnson and "turning now and then a couplet in my translation of
Michel Angelo's Sonnets. I was not fit for work." Later that year
he began to feel "impelled to write that series of my Sonnets which
are called 'Sonnets on the Thought of Death' ", according to Brown
From 1877 to 1882 Symonds wrote most of the sonnets in Animi
Figura and Vagabunduli Libellus. When he showed the whole array
to Robert Louis Stevenson, a newcomer to Davos Platz in 1882,
he was delighted with the "glad appreciation which Stevenson and
his wife have given my sonnets. . . . They are enthusiastic about
the dialectical ones."(9) In fact, the title is the suggestion of
Stevenson, "one whose literary tact and judgment helped to form
this Animi Figura,"(10) and the selective principle of choosing
only those sonnets that prefigure a mind provided Symonds with
a unifying theme. "It is an odd book; but it is all of one sort."(11)

What Symonds meant by "an odd book" he attempts to explain
in the preface. After warning the reader that "this Portrait of a
Mind is not a piece of accurate self-delineation", he turns to the
central question about all sonnet sequences: "whether the sonnet
can be appropriately used as a stanza in poems which demand
suspension of the reader's mind over the more or less prolonged
development of some one motive".

Symonds' answer is that where the material warrants there is
justification for "extending a single train of thought from one sonnet to another in such wise that the point developed in a preceding
sonnet is necessary to the comprehension of its successor". In
defense of this position he cites the Italian "sequences of Folgore
da San Gemignano, Campanella's triad on the Lord's Prayer, and
Onofrio Minzoni's fine series on the Death of Sampson". Yet,
Symonds acknowledges that "Italian precedent" is not so valid a

justification as "the nature of the sonnet itself". Citing fourteen
lines and the equipoise between the two parts of the stanza as the
essential feature of the sonnet, Symonds concludes that "in the
conduct of a lengthy argument sonnet may succeed to sonnet, pro-
pounding and disputing themes which need for their development
the thesis and antithesis of logical discussion".

Symonds would probably not have approved Swinburne's use of
the sonnet in certain scenes of Locrine, where only the rhythm
and rime scheme are preserved, the sonnet having become a mere
strophe. (12) Symonds does, however, judge "Rossetti's Willow
Wood" (later to become a part of The House of Life) as the acme
of sonnet grouping in English: "The continuous argument has been
so ordered that each step is presented in a separate and self-
sufficient poem. The sonnet has not passed into a strophé."
Symonds' practical answer to the dilemma of the sonnet sequence
was a via media between Swinburne and Rossetti, using a variety
of linking devices between single sonnet entities. For Symonds,
at least in Animi Figura, "the sonnet is essentially a meditative
lyric". (13) He would have agreed with C. S. Lewis that after
Petrarch abandoned the practice of prose links between sonnet
groupings that Dante and others had used, the sonnet sequence
should not be considered "a way of telling a story". (14)

Symonds' practice in Animi Figura illustrates the theory he pro-
pounds in the preface. The volume is in reality a sequence of sequences. And since each of the sequences bears an individual title,
the composite effect of the titles is a sort of vestigial remain of
the earlier Italian practice of prose links. Three of the twenty-
one titled groupings (excluding "A Dedication") are each composed
of one sonnet: "The Temptation of Adam", "Revolt", and "O, Si!
O, Si!" Each of these sonnets is entirely understandable in its own
right, yet each takes on a fuller meaning when read in its sequential
place in the description of the artist—"speculative rather than
creative"—whose mind is prefigured in the whole volume.

When the grouping consists of two sonnets, however, Symonds'
intended stanzaic effect becomes clear. In "Personality" the second
sonnet begins "Yes, both shall carry with them to the void / Without, the void more terrible within". The antecedent of "both"
("lovers") comes solely from the first sonnet, whose central theme
is that men can never know themselves or each other. Yet when
the second sonnet is read alone, it does succeed in conveying its
theme: even God cannot be known. Its reader would subsume an
indefinite both, somewhat equivalent to "men in general". It

might even be said of the poem when read separately that it achieves an intriguing vagueness in its beginning that contrasts with the precise imagery of the concluding lines: "Or if each impulse, wild as wind at play, / Be but a cog-wheel in the cosmic plan." When the grouping consists of more than two sonnets, Symonds' methods of linking are more various. In the opening sequence "The Innovators" the first three sonnets begin "Woe unto", "Woe unto", and "Woe to", and the fourth opens with "And yet". The fifth sonnet, beginning "Is he sage, madman, malefactor, fool", uses the pronoun "he" to point back to the "innovator" and forward to a generalized "he . . . who sets his dauntless intellect to school". The latter device Symonds probably learned from Rossetti, who was so skillful with pronominal reference that The House of Life sonnets seem, in Symonds' words in the preface, "linked together by a chain so delicate that severance is almost mutilation". The emphasis is on "almost", for when severance does take place the pronouns point in a different direction or become generalized to the indefinite.

On the other hand, the eleven sonnets of "Debate on Self" are so closely linked that they can be read separately with only partial understanding. In the eleventh sonnet, for example, "The triune amulet whereof I speak" is not defined except in the preceding sonnet as "Faith, Hope, and Charity". A similar closeness of linking can be seen in the three sonnets of "Paths of Life". The first recounts the argument of a friend: marriage sanctifies love by giving it permanence even though "love can blow / But rarely". The second sonnet, like a sestet to the first, begins: "I take both points, and answer: . . . you misread / Marriage and comradeship." And the third sonnet summarizes and synthesizes the two points of view: "We all are wanderers", and therefore comradeship has a mystic binding power beyond that of marriage. Still another example of Symonds' method of close linking occurs in "An Old Gordian Knot", a group of eight sonnets on the Arnoldian theme of modern faith ("we who, knowing, yet know naught"). Here the sequence is held together by the figure of the Alpine mists that are described in the second sonnet. The third begins: "Then in my soul I cried: even such is God". And the remaining sonnets adumbrate the symbol of the clear empyrean that is God and the mists that veil him from man who through the ages must continue "Storming Olympus".

This variety of close linking can be contrasted with the twenty-two sonnets in "The Thought of Death", which are bound together only by title; rearrangement in the ordering does little injustice to the whole. In this same vein Symonds sometimes assigns individual titles to each sonnet. In "L'Amour de l'impossible" the first sonnet is called "Proemium", the second "The Furies", the third "Chimaera", and the fourth "The Pursuit of Beauty". To some extent these titles act as comments, supplying in brief the kind of prose link used by Dante in the Vita Nuova. Without the titles the arrangement would seem as loose as that in "The Thought of Death".

Though one cannot make a case for Animi Figura as a work of poetic power, it should be noted that Symonds has created one of the longer English sequence of sequences in the meditative as opposed to the amatory tradition in which most of the English poets before him had worked. For him it was a part of his therapy as he set about to make a new life for himself in Switzerland. For the development of the sonnet sequence in English Animi Figura is the most interesting work in the meditative tradition since Wordsworth, and it began a renaissance of the medium in the last decade of the century by poets like Wilfrid Scawen Blunt, William Watson, and Eugene Lee-Hamilton.

(B)

After the publication of Animi Figura Symonds, who needed things to do while he waited for research material from England and Italy for his Renaissance studies, reached into his "vast and well-filled 'desolation box'"(15) to resurrect the sonnets that had not appealed to the Stevensons. Having changed publishers from Smith, Elder to Kegan Paul, Symonds returned to his original title of Vagabunduli Libellus since, according to the preface, "all men on this earth are wanderers". Between the lines of this introductory comment, it seems apparent that Symonds was looking for almost any excuse to restore his "Venetian series" to its rightful place — a place that did not appeal to the recently married Stevensons. At any rate, Symonds puts a diplomatic face on the matter, and states in the preface: "I wrote ['Stella Maris'] to supplement and to explain what is defective and unintelligible in a collection of sonnets called Animi Figura, published by me in 1882. 'Stella Maris' forms in fact the transition from 'Intellectual Isolation' to 'Self-Condemnation' in that book."

The sequence of sixty-seven sonnets opens in a tone of deep

melancholy; the speaker is contemplating the "last miseries of
mankind . . . loves that know themselves shameful and blind".
In the second sonnet he catches a glimpse of the lady for the first
time near Venice on the Lido; it is love at first sight. There
follows a group of rapturous sonnets descriptive of Venice,
"Roofed with that crystal dome of luminous sky", and of his own
true Stella Maris foam-born from the sea. For some thirty
sonnets the narrator worships her from afar, fascinated by her
eyes and imagining her vain and cruel. In his imagination he de-
mands her to yield herself to him, yet he realizes that "souls
sequestered" such as theirs will never be one. Even though she
causes him mental and physical torment, he knows that he is
wholly hers. It is not, however, until Sonnet XXXV that the actual
meeting of the lovers takes place:

> It came at length, our meeting. Her white dress,
>   Those summer robes she then so lightly wore,
>   Were changed for winter's livery, and the shore
> Of Lido where she stood, now 'neath the stress
> Of rude Borrin with wavelets numberless
>   Moaned to grey lands and cloud-capped mountains hoar.

The climax of the sequence begins with a description of the lady's
bedroom: "Silvery mosquito-curtains draped the bed: / A lamp
stood on the table". As he "drank her lips; as thirsty flowers
drink rain". he imagines that "Love cried: Less than Love's best
thou shalt refuse". As the lovers lie side by side and watch the
ascendant day, Scorn seems to say:

> There neither is, nor can there ever be,
> 'Twixt that white body and thy weak heart's desire,
> Communion.

The remaining sonnets are the narrator's outbursts against himself and the lady. He is in quest of an ideal love and only half
realizes that "These longings are / Mere madness, like to theirs
who clasp a star". In Sonnet XLV he exclaims to the lady:

> Take it, oh take it, take thy gold! the shame
>   Shall rest with me, the bitter barren bliss
>   Of dreaming on a joy so brief as this.
> Thou hast no suffering, and, I think, no blame.

The lady flees, and in a fit of remorse he accuses his will of playing him false. In his dreams he sees himself and love together in harmony of mind and body. Finally, he learns that Stella has gone mad, and in a measure he is comforted, for now she too is separated from "life's common lot"; he finds solace in the fact that "we both have fallen, but God is great". Stella is mad, and his love too was madness' very self. At last comes the final resolution of his consolation:

> Where God is, I am, and Thou art. The cost
>> Shall not be counted, when at length in Him
>> Both blend, as blend we must, spirit and limb.

Sonnets LXIII-LXVII form an epilogue, shifting from the first to the third person, which suggests that from a "trivial act" may arise nobility of thought and "healthy flesh newborn, exhilarated" for "This man, whose impotence shows manifest / In the cold light of life's philosophy".

As a sequence in the narrative tradition of Shakespeare, Mrs. Browning, Meredith, or Rossetti, "Stella Maris" is not entirely successful. Symonds, who seems partially aware of its shortcomings, writes in the preface:

> To tell a story in a series of sonnets, is no easy task, because the effort to do so puts a severe strain upon the law whereby the sonnet lives. That form of verse is not designed for continuous narration, but for the crystallization of thought, meditation, or remembrance. I have therefore omitted from "Stella Maris" such connecting links as ought assuredly to have been supplied if this love-episode had been presented in prose or idyll, or in any of the numerous types of narrative verse.

In fact, the chief weakness of "Stella Maris" is this matter of "connecting links", which Symonds has not really omitted: "It came at length, our meeting" (XXXV), "And then she rose" (XXXVIII), "She then is flown" (XLVII), "they write me, Stella, write me thou art mad" (LII). These links are too prosily obvious in a sequence that metrically aims at the integrity of the individual sonnet as opposed to a stanzaic concept. Symonds is unwilling to allow the narrative line to remain implied amid the sonnets of lyric meditation as do Shakespeare and Mrs. Browning. He is not satisfied with a sequence of moods like that of The House of Life, nor does he seem aware of Meredith's technique in <u>Modern Love</u>, where narrative scenes are dramatized at key points throughout the sequence. Perhaps the failure of his compromise lies in the larger failure of his doctrine of <u>sincerity</u> put to too great a test in this poem. Stella is the fictional disguise of the gondolier Angelo Fusato; the poem was written almost immediately after a similarly real episode had occurred. By this shift in sex the emotions of the introverted and self-centered hero that seem to him overpowering are actually in excess of the central situation in the poem.(16) In his private letters Symonds acknowledges this fault: to his sister Charlotte he apologizes for the "too spasmodic" quality, and to his friend Agnes Mary Robinson he wrote: "As for people not believing my preface it will be very nasty of them if they don't", (17) as though "belief" were germane to the problem he failed to solve.

It is usually impossible to explain why a man of intellect and passion who very much wants to be a poet cannot quite succeed. Perhaps one reason that Symonds' sonnets seem relatively cold and lifeless is that his own criterion was not aesthetic but moral – the criterion of <u>sincerity</u>. Though as critic Symonds used many touchstones in evaluating the work of other poets, for himself as poet there was but one: <u>sincerity</u> — at least for the writer. But Symonds seems never to have asked himself how the poem would seem to the reader. In his well-known review of Rossetti's <u>House of Life</u> (i.e., <u>New Poems</u>), for example, Symonds refers to the sonnets as "cabinet productions" because they lack any evidence of real and personal suffering:(18) Symonds never gives evidence of comprehending that essential of good lyric poetry which Rossetti called "fundamental brainwork" — a process that leads to compression and ultimately to that magic which A.E. Housman says would make him cut himself while shaving. When one reads Symonds' descriptive prose about winter in Davos or spring in Venice, one realizes that his poetry on the same subjects is little different, being merely metered, rimed, and arranged. As early as 1862 Symonds was generally aware of this fault though he was never able to pinpoint it: "I am discontented, because I do not feel myself a poet, and do not see why I should not be one."(19)

Symonds' second fault grows out of this criterion of <u>sincerity</u>. Since "the problem" of his life was homosexuality, (20) it follows naturally that much of his poetry concerns this subject. In short, poetry became for him a kind of therapy, wherein he could examine a facet of his personality that he could acknowledge only to certain of his intimate friends. But when it came to publication, he would allow his literary friends like Graham Dakyns or the brothers Sidgwick to decide what could and could not be published, what must be changed and to what extent. For example, in the first sonnet of "The Alps and Italy"—"I had two loves"—the line "Or she whose mouth mixed passion like a cup" was "Or he whose mouth" in the privately printed Rhaetica according to Grosskurth. And the inspirer of "Stella Maris" was not a Venetian prostitute, but rather the gondolier Angelo Fusato.(21) Thus, much of Symonds' poetry is cloaked in a false apparel that even belies his own doctrine of sincerity.

The very failure of Symonds' sequential technique in "Stella Maris", however, is something of a landmark. It was inevitable after Modern Love that experiments in further blending the narrative and lyric in the sonnet series would occur. And "Stella Maris" made possible the more fully realized sequences of the nineties like Blunt's Esther and Natalia's Resurrection, which in turn foreshadowed the work of William Ellery Leonard in Two Lives (1925) and John Berryman in Berryman's Sonnets (1967). Though Symonds' other sonnet groupings in Vagabunduli Libellus show no techniques of sonnet linking beyond those discussed in Animi Figura, experiments with individual sonnets are often interesting and effective, like the imitation of the meter of the Venetian vilota in Sonnet IV of "Stella Maris":

Fair is the sea; and fair the sea-borne billow,
Blue from the depth and curled with crested argent.
Fair is the sea; and fair the smooth sea-margent
The brown dunes waved with tamarisk and willow.

(C)

Symonds' major contributions to the genre of the sonnet sequence are at least three. By the device of a spiritual autobiography(22)—an animi figura—he created a sequence of sequences that provides a prelude to one human mind. By varying the length of the groups of Animi Figura from two to twenty-two sonnets, by using titles for each grouping and by entitling the single sonnets, he avoids some of the monotony inherent in sonnet series. Second, by the close linking of certain sonnets Symonds has been able to demonstrate the strength of his medium for long arguments without the obtruding prose links that Wordsworth used when Sonnets upon the Punishment of Death first appeared in the Quarterly Review.

Symonds has maintained the integrity of the sonnet while pushing
the verse form to its limits as it approaches stanzaic character.
To avoid such a problem Wordsworth usually confined his meditative sequences to some simple plan: the course of a river from
source to sea like The River Duddon: A Series of Sonnets, or a
walking tour like Yarrow Revisited (composed predominantly of
sonnets), or historical chronology like Ecclesiastical Sonnets.
Wordsworth once commented to Sir Henry Taylor: "Where I
have a large amount of Sonnets in series, I have not been unwilling to start sometimes with a logical connective of a 'Yet'
or a 'But'."(23) Symonds has gone further: "Many of the sequences
in Animi Figura . . . [extend] a single train of thought from one
sonnet to another in such wise that the point developed in a preceding sonnet is necessary to the comprehension of its successor.
(24) And third, Symonds' very failure in "Stella Maris" to find a
suitable technique for linking sonnets in a narrative of some
complication of plot suggested that the long series was still
vital and viable for further experimentation.

Symonds' sensible comments about the sonnet and the sonnet
sequence were a welcome relief to much of the foolish and petty
"sonnet Legislation" that became a sort of sad critical cult of
"legitimacy" and "canonization" in the closing years of the century. (25) After pointing out that "the English sonnet is no longer
. . . an exotic from Italy . . . and has assumed a character ac-
cordant with the English genius", and that "great varieties in
the structure of the sonnet have come to be accepted as equally
legitimate", Symonds makes his most telling point: "To tell a
story in a series of sonnets is no easy task, because the effort
to do so puts a severe strain upon the law whereby the sonnet
lives."(26)

Finally, in the prefaces to both Animi Figura and Vagabunduli
Libellus Symonds is probably the first poet-critic to comment on
the term "sonnet sequence" and to suggest a saner critical approach to the sonnet in general. After Rossetti entitled The House
of Life "A Sonnet-Sequence" in the 1881 edition of his poems, the
term was picked up by Symonds. Later it was used by Swinburne,
Blunt, and Watts-Dunton, from whence it passed into common
currency. It is now applied in criticism to all sonnet groupings,
though no major poet used the term before Rossetti and no poet-
critic discussed it before Symonds. As sonneteer and critic of
the sonnet, John Addington Symonds deserves credit for at least
this much.

NOTES

(1) The Letters of John Addington Symonds, 1844-1893, ed.
Herbert Schueller and Robert Peters (Detroit: Wayne State Univ.
Press, 1967-69). Unfortunately, of these 2113 letters only the
first volume was available to me in the preparation of this essay
(hereafter cited as Letters).
(2) This was the decision of Symonds' literary executor, Horatio
F. Brown, who at the time of his death in 1926 placed a fifty-
year prohibition against the publication of the memoirs deposited
in the London Library. His own bowdlerized selections from the
autobiography and letters were first issued in 1895 as his John
Addington Symonds, A Biography, and his partially collected
Letters and Papers of John Addington Symonds appeared in 1923.
Van Wyck Brooks in his John Addington Symonds, A Biographical
Study (1914) makes no use of the autobiographical memoir, which
forms the basis (though it could not be quoted) of Phyllis
Grosskurth's excellent 1964 biography of Symonds, The Woeful
Victorian.
(3) Phyllis Grosskurth, The Woeful Victorian, A Biography of
John Addington Symonds (New York: Holt, 1964), p. 28 (hereafter
cited as Grosskurth).
(4) Horatio F. Brown, John Addington Symonds, A Biography,
2nd ed. (London, 1903), p. 78 (hereafter cited as Brown).
(5) MS letter of December 1872, quoted in Grosskurth, p. 151.
(6) Symonds also printed in 1878 a few copies of frankly homo-
sexual poems called Rhaetica, somewhat in imitation of Whitman's
Calamus poems. Some of the individual poems appeared in later
volumes with the pronouns altered from masculine to the feminine. For a discussion of these sexually metamorphosized poems —
some published and some unpublished — see Robert L. Peters,
"Athens and Troy: Notes on John Addington Symonds' Aestheticism",
English Fiction in Transition, 5 (1962), 14-26.
(7) Letter to his sister Charlotte, quoted in Grosskurth, p. 195.
(8) John Addington Symonds, A Biographical Study (London:
Grant Richards, 1914), p. 150.
(9) Letter of March [1882], quoted in Brown, pp. 330, 370.
(10) Preface, p. vii.
(11) Brown, p. 370.
(12) Though Symonds respected Swinburne as a poet, it is doubtful that he read the drama Locrine, for he had decided as early
as 1867 that Swinburne was "more than usually verbose. . . .

He does not attend to the projection of his thought enough, but splashes it out as if he were upsetting a bucket" (Letter to Henry Sidgwick, November 17, 1867, Schuller and Peters, Letters, I, 776).

(13) This quotation, as well as the other undocumented ones in the preceding two paragraphs, is taken from the preface of Animi Figura.

(14) English Literature in the Sixteenth Century (Oxford: Clarendon Press, 1954), p. 327 (see "The Modernity of Modern Love", p. 113).

(15) Letter "to a young friend who was failing at the start", quoted in Brown, p. 376.

(16) For a discussion of Symonds' relationship with Angelo Fusato, see Grosskurth, pp. 241-242.

(17) MS. letter, November 9, 1884, quoted in Grosskurth, p. 218; MS. letter, November 14, 1884, quoted in Grosskurth, p. 242n.

(18) "Notes on Mr. Rossetti's New Poems", Macmillan's Magazine, XLV (February, 1882), 325.

(19) Brown, p. 142.

(20) This is the well-documented thesis of Mrs. Grosskurth's biographical study.

(21) Mrs. Grosskurth's and Schueller and Peters' spelling is Fusato, while both Brown and Brooks write Fusatto.

(22) Though Symonds in the preface denies any autobiography, one must agree in the main with Van Wyck Brooks that "[Animi Figura] is indeed the real Symonds, hidden from his generation" (Brooks, p. 151).

(23) The Letters of William and Dorothy Wordsworth: The Later Years, ed. Ernest de Selincourt (Oxford: Clarendon Press, 1939), III, 1097.

(24) Preface, p. ix.

(25) The attitudes of this cult are evident in the following: Capel Lofft's Laura; Or an Anthology of Sonnets, (on the Petrarcan Model) (1814), Charles Tomlinson's The Sonnet: Its Origin, Structure, and Place in Poetry (1874), David M. Main's A Treasury of English Sonnets (1880), T. Hall Caine's Sonnets of Three Centuries (1882), and finally in an oddly intemperate work that defines a sonnet sequence as "a sonnet surfeit", T. W. H. Crosland's The English Sonnet (1917).

(26) Animi Figura, preface, p. ix; Vagabunduli Libellus, preface, p. ix.

7. WILFRID SCAWEN BLUNT: THE SUMMARY OF A TRADITION

(A)

Wilfrid Scawen Blunt (1840-1922) was many things to many men.
To the distinguished painter G.F. Watts, despite the fact that
he never instructed students, the fourteen-year-old Wilfrid was
promising enough for the artist to agree to take the boy as a
pupil. (1) Later Blunt's interest in art was one of the chief bonds
of his friendship with William Morris. And like Morris, Blunt
had a craftsman's interest in all the graphic and plastic arts:
for the tomb of his elder brother, Wilfrid carved a recumbent
figure of Francis in a friar's habit; for the Egyptian grave of his
wife, the daughter of Byron's Ada, he designed and drew to scale
an elaborate monument; and for The Love Sonnets of Proteus
(1881 edition) he sketched his own pen and ink frontispiece.
   To Dr. Charles Meynell and Cardinal Manning, Blunt was a
troubled, somewhat brash young aristocrat who needed Catholic
guidance to quell the doubts raised by Darwin's Origin of Species.
So striking was the correspondence between Blunt and Meynell
that Aubrey de Vere edited it in 1878 as a remarkable record of
young doubt and old faith: Proteus and Amadeus, A Correspondence.
   To the British Foreign Office, Blunt was, beginning in 1858,
an unpaid attaché who was shifted from Athens to Constantinople,
Germany, the Argentine, Paris, and in 1865 to Lisbon, where he
met the young, popular writer–diplomat, Robert Lytton. To
"Owen Meredith" Wilfrid had "great gifts to keep or cast away".
Even after his resignation in 1869 the Foreign Office was well
aware of Scawen Blunt, who bitterly and publicly attacked its
exploiting, imperialistic policies in the letter columns of the
Times, in journals like the Fortnightly and Nineteenth Century,
in pamphlets, and in a series of six volumes, known later as his
Secret History Series. Winston Churchill, a young friend of Blunt,
once remarked to the journalist T.P. O'Connor that Blunt's political purpose seemed to be "the breakup of the British Empire".
To the English reading public of the closing years of the nineteenth century until his death in 1922 Blunt, the world traveler
and personal historian and diarist, was the unofficial liberal

conscience of a growing empire. With his time, energy, and
wealth he fought with Byronic glamor the forces of intolerance
and oppression on three continents.

To the smaller world of Ireland in 1888 Blunt was a public
hero who dared challenge the rights of English landlords and who
single-handed almost succeeded in overthrowing Balfour's Irish
policy. Blunt was the first Englishman to go to prison for the
dispossessed Irish farmers. (2) To even the smaller world of
Deptford and Kidderminster he was a colorful but unsuccessful
Liberal candidate for Parliament (having refused several Irish
constituencies). And to the people of southern England he was
the owner of some three hundred acres and two fine houses,
Crabbet Park and Newbuildings Place, where he was more than
a country squire—a sort of "uncrowned king of Sussex", who
greeted his guests in flowing Arab robes.

To men like E. M. Forster, T. E. Lawrence, and Charles
Doughty, who knew the wide world of East and West, Blunt "had
the power of alluring the East. . . . He lives in its unwritten
chronicles as one of the few really noble Englishmen."(3) To
sportsmen and Arab horse fanciers the annual sale from the
Crabbet Park stud was a gala and fashionable affair, the invi-
tations to which were much sought after and highly prized.

Finally, to those interested in belles-lettres Blunt was the
author of a verse novel, a drama produced at the Abbey Theatre,
and a dozen volumes of poetry extending from 1875 to 1914—
from the Sonnets and Songs by Proteus to the Poetical Works in
two volumes. A many-sided Victorian with an Elizabethan ex-
pansiveness of curiosity, Blunt wrote some of his best poetry in
the sonnet form, and his six sequences, published during the
last two decades of the nineteenth century, illustrate and summarize the principal traditions of the nineteenth-century sonnet
sequence; they suggest that this medium, as he employs it, is
more flexible than it appeared to any one of his more famous
contemporaries. Furthermore, of the 330 sonnets in his Poetical
Works 271 are parts of sequences, and editors and anthologists
have been of the consistent opinion that his memorable sonnets
are those in sequences.

Although Blunt was not a major poet even in his own day, his
verse was seriously reviewed. The Love Sonnets of Proteus
(1888) went through at least seven editions, and at the close of
the century his poetry was prefaced, selected, and arranged by
W. E. Henley and George Wyndham (both of whom Blunt outlived

to re-arrange his own Poetical Works sixteen years later). The younger generation of poets admired Blunt the man and his spirit as much as his verse. At a testimonial dinner given for him by Pound, Yeats, Masefield, and others in 1914, Pound began his address:

> Because you have gone your individual gait,
> Written fine verse, made mock of the world,
> Swung the grand style, not made a trade of art,
> Upheld Mazzini and detested institutions. . . .

Blunt was horrified on this occasion to see that they had confused Mazzini with Arabi, the Egyptian leader whom he admired, and they, in turn, were embarrassed by Blunt's conservative notions of versification and by his poor opinion of modern poets. (4)

In the same year Blunt had probably gauged his own measure when in the preface to his Poetical Works he called himself "a mid-Victorian poet a little in advance of his epoch". If he had been asked to explain precisely what he meant, Blunt would probably have suggested, as he had in the preface to A New Pilgrimage in 1889, that, among other things, he had broadened the scope of the sonnet, especially the imitations of the "strict Petrarchan measure which are . . . intolerably dull", and insisted upon "modern subjects". Unlike Lord Alfred Douglas and Sir William Watson, who at the turn of the century were still imitating Petrarch in modulations that echoed both the Elizabethans and Rossetti, Blunt had experimented vigorously with the form and content of the sonnet, particularly within the traditions of the sonnet sequence.

No other poet in the nineteenth century used a greater variety of subject matter in sequences or employed more varied methods to organize these sequences into unified poems than did Blunt. Mrs. Browning, the Rossettis, Meredith, and Bridges wrote greater sequences, but their interest in the genre extended little beyond the amatory tradition. Wordsworth, who wrote more sonnets in sequence than any other major English poet, wrote no sequence in the amatory tradition. Swinburne's most memorable poetry is not in his sonnet sequences. And John Addington Symonds, Blunt's most prolific compeer, composed no single sequence that can compare in organic unity with Esther.

(B)

Like The House of Life and The Growth of Love, The Love Sonnets of Proteus had a slow evolution. To trace its growth would
require an examination of six versions—from a "little volume
of mixed verse and prose" of 1867 that was rejected by George
Meredith as reader for Chapman & Hall to The Love Sonnets of
Proteus in the Poetical Works of 1914. The very length of the
poems varied markedly, from 36 sonnets in Sonnets and Songs
(1875) to 141 in Morris's Kelmscott edition (1892). (5) Unlike
The House of Life, however, the Proteus sonnets have a philosophic unity not present in Rossetti's poem. Unlike that of The
Growth of Love the unity is implicit in the organization of the
poem, unmetaphysical and sharply defined. The variety of
methods used to obtain this central unity can be seen most clearly by an examination of the way the subject matter of the four
parts is developed in small segments and linked into larger wholes
    Part I, "To Manon", contains in the final edition twenty-one
sonnets. The three added in 1892 (XII, XIII, and XXI) mark the
breaks in the arrangement. The first ten (II-XI) are addressed to
Manon; they form a closely integrated unit, not one of the ten
having appeared in Sonnets and Songs (1875). By adopting the
fiction of Manon, Blunt echoes the Elizabethan convention of
stylized names for a mistress, and at the same time suggests
the atmosphere of Prévost's "pastoral" with Proteus changed
for the moment to a Des Grieux. "I have loved too much, too
loyally, too long", he exclaims in Sonnet XXI. The first five
sonnets, which praise the charm and fascination of Manon, can
be interchanged as can the last five, which emphasize her vanity,
her waywardness, and her heartless playing with the hearts of
men. The ten sonnets to the beauty and fatality of Manon are
linked by antithetical refrains and repetitive phrases. Though
indulging in Elizabethan conceits, the controlling imagery of
Part I is Biblical. Sonnet III links Love's altar to the Pauline
account of the Athenian dedication "To the unknown god"; in Sonnet VI Proteus becomes an Old Testament prophet crying, "Be
these your gods, O Israel!" In Sonnet XI he longs for Manon's
heartless "Peace passing understanding" that "Like David with
washed face" he may cease to weep.
    The last ten sonnets of Part I are about Manon instead of to
Manon. They are miscellaneous and retrospective. Proteus
would rise up on Horeb and cry, "There is none other god, but

only I". In the last sonnet "His Bondage to Manon Is Broken".
The point of view returns dramatically to Manon, but the theme
is perspective regret:

> From this day forth I lead another life, . . .
> Let others love, and love as tenderly.
> Oh, Manon, there are women yet unborn
> Shall rue thy frailty, else am I forsworn.

And with Shakespearean rhetoric on this tongue Proteus turns to
a new love, Juliet.

The pattern of organization of Part I is that of theme and variation—the theme of the fatal fascination of Manon in the first
ten, variations on the effects of that love in the last ten. In Part
II the reverse is true. The last fifteen — all under the title of
"Farewell to Juliet"—afford closely unified lyric glimpses of
lovers of disparate ages who struggle to sustain the passion of
first infatuation. The first seventeen are variations upon such
a love. The philosophy of love is again the fascination and power
of sensual joys, but the grouping of sonnets in quartets and trios
suggests an underlying narrative. The narrative, like that in
Sonnets from the Portuguese is a simple one but different in out-
come. Here the "story" is of physical passion yielded to and the
subsequent reproach and jealousy. The climax of the more miscellaneous opening group of seventeen comes in Sonnet XXVIII:

> Why should I hate you, love, or why despise
> For that last proof of tenderness you gave?
> The battle is not always to the brave,
> Nor life's sublimest wisdom to the wise.

The climax of the fifteen "Farewell" sonnets (three of which are
constructed with the "flashback" technique of narrative: "Do you
remember how . . .") comes in Sonnet XLIII:

> I do not love . . . I, no less than you,
> Here own at length the worm which cannot die,
> The burden of a pain for ever new.

And Part II ends with the surprise denouement:

> See, I came to curse,

Yet stay to bless. I know not which is worse.

Though Manon and Juliet have much in common, the latter is far
more real than the more universal Manon. Juliet has blue eyes;
when Proteus first knew that he loved her, she wore a white
muslin dress, a _fischu_ trimmed with lace, and a red rose at her
bosom. Juliet is thirty; she is a "woman with a past". Yet she
has regrets and even blushes "that we have been / One day in
Eden in our nakedness". She is both Victorian Cyprian and Victorian maiden and wife.

Just as the first parts of the Proteus sonnets form complementary sections, so do the last two, "Gods and False Gods" and
"Vita Nova". Both present a variety of subject matter. Instead
of alternating patterns of theme and variation, the principle of
organization seems to be the everbroadening facets of new loves
and substitutes for love, with restrospective glimpses at those
past moments of great passion. Almost all the sonnets of Part
III except the last and the six composing the two trios, "The
Three Ages of Woman" and "The Mockery of Life", can be interchanged. Themes of love and its flatness naturally lead to reflections on time and death. But this effect is not ordered; it is
merely cumulative. The first sonnet (LIV), "He Desires the
Impossible", is Elizabethan in its conceits, imagery, and diction,
recalling the tone of Part I:

> If it were possible the fierce sun should,
> Standing in heaven unloved, companionless,
>
> Enshrinèd be in some white-bosomed cloud,
> And so forget the rage and loneliness;
> If it were possible the bitter seas. . . .

The second sonnet (LV), "St. Valentine's Day", recalls the exhil-
aration of the moment of sensual love that to Proteus excels any
power of spiritual happiness — the central idea of Part II:

> Your face my quarry was. For it I rode,
> My horse a thing of wings, myself a god.

In the last sonnet (LXXXII), "He Would Lead a Better Life",
Proteus intimates the futility of expecting figs from thistles:

I am tired of folly, tired of my own ways,
Love is a strife. . . .
I would do this, dear love. But what am I
To will or do? As we have lived we die.

The arrangement of Part IV, "Vita Nova", is similar to that of
Part III. The new life for Proteus is heralded by an increasing
love for the land as exemplified in the opening sonnet, "Day in
Sussex" (LXXXIII), and repeated in "Chanclebury Ring" (XCVII).
This love of land is extended to love for all England in "Gibraltar"
(CXII), for the paradise of Eastern deserts in "The Oasis of Sid
Khaled" (CX), and for the whole natural earth that is "in very
truth . . . too young". Some sonnets also recall memories of
family travel, like "Palazzo Pagani", and of the death of a loved
one, like the elegiac sequence of five to Francis, "In Anni-
versario Mortis" (LXXXIV-LXXXVIII). Part IV, in short, concerns the memories and interests that fill Proteus' maturing
life.

Blunt's love for many women went into the creation of Proteus'
changing loves. But across his whole life, particularly before
his marriage and after the death of Lady Anne, as across the
whole of the Proteus sonnets, falls the shadow of Catherine
Walters, familiarly known to the fashionable world as "Skittles".
(6) One of the most renowned beauties and courtesans of the
latter part of the nineteenth century, she was a friend of Edward
VII, Gladstone, Lord Clarincarde, Lord Hartington, Lord
Kitchener, and others. Catherine Walters might be given the
name of Manon, Juliet, or Esther; she might lurk behind gods
and false gods and even behind a new life; but she always symbolizes the guiding "clouds" and "pillars of fire"—for "The
wilderness is long". In Paris in 1863 Blunt first saw her, and
in 1920, after a lifetime of devoted friendship, when she died
at the advanced age of eighty-one, he succeeded in having her
buried in the churchyard of the Crawley Fathers at the monastery
founded on his estate in Sussex.

From the evolution of the poem as well as from this account
of its structure, it is evident that the poem has variety above all
things. The sonnets themselves range from thirteen to twenty
lines in length;(7) some are separately titled, others grouped in
gatherings extending from two to fifteen lyrics. The point of
view likewise varies between immediate urgency and restrained
recollection. From 1881 to 1914 Blunt experimented with giving

the poem greater unity within its original variety, chiefly by the process of adding and deleting sonnets. By leaving the core of his work unchanged in its metrics, he manages to keep the tone of restrained urgency that Rossetti loses in the process of re-working his sonnets line by line and image by image. By so doing, Blunt loses much in poetic compression and often fails in creating a lyric line of the first rank, but he manages always to convey a poetic sense of a natural clear-sighted analysis of his Protean self.

The Love Sonnets of Proteus does not have the unity of mood and tone of The House of Life, nor the neo-metaphysical power of The Growth of Love, nor the clarity of emotional climaxes of Sonnets from the Portuguese, nor the compact, dramatic subtlety of Modern Love. The unique quality of Blunt's sequence, the longest of the Victorian sequences in the amatory tradition, is that it manages, through employing almost all the methods of the amatory-lyric sequence in its various parts of immediate passion and impassioned recollection, to create the cumulative effect of a unified poem that is sincere in tone, real in subject matter, and broad and changing in scope.

Esther treats the same material as the "To Manon" section of Proteus, but from a more narrative perspective. In fact, Esther is a thrice-told tale, having been originally written in the 1860's as a blank verse poem. (8) The difference in the two works can be best illustrated by a sonnet from each.

DEPRECIATING HER BEAUTY [SONNET VI, PROTEUS]

> I love not thy perfections. When I hear
> Thy beauty blazoned, and the common tongue
> Cheapening with vulgar praise a lip, an ear,
> A cheek that I have prayed to;—when among
> The loud world's gods my god is noised and sung,
> Her wit applauded, even her taste, her dress,
> Her each dear hidden marvel lightly flung
> At the world's feet and stripped to nakedness —
> Then I despise thy beauty utterly
> Crying, "Be these your gods, O Israel!"
> And I remember that on such a day
> I found thee with eyes bleared and cheeks all pale,
> And that thy bosom in my bosom lay.

LV [ESTHER]

We stayed at Lyons three days, only three,
  In Esther's world of wonder and renown.
She, glorious star, each night immortally,
  Playing her Manons to the listening town.
I glorious too, but in Love's firmament,
  Watching her face by which alone I moved,
A shadow near her raptured and intent,
  And seeking still the signs that I was loved.
Thrice happy days! Thrice blessed tragedy!
  Her Des Grieux was I, her lover lorn
Bound to her fortunes, blest to live or die,
  And faithful ever though to faith forsworn.
Waiting behind the scenes in that stage-land
To greet her exits and to squeeze her hand. (9)

The emotion expressed in the two poems is similar, but the
Proteus sonnet is generalized, whereas the Esther sonnet is precisely detailed. In the former Manon could be a popular courtesan,
a fabulous horse-woman admired by the masculine crowds in
Rotten Row, as was Skittles in real life, or she could equally well
be an actress like Rachel. The "To Manon" sonnets form a collection of lyrics with a central theme — Proteus's passionate love
for a cruel mistress; the Esther sonnets are "the tale I have to
tell".
  The first four sonnets of Esther form an introduction on the
pervasive nature of tragedy in the entire span of human life and
establish a point of view for the narration. The opening of Sonnet
V, however, is abrupt and pointedly narrative — the story has
begun in medias res: "I had been an hour at Lyons". This section
(Sonnets V-XXI) recounts the circumstances of the first meeting
with "a little woman dressed in black". The place is the Lyons
fair in a side-show tent; the time is dusk. As the speaker watches
two "female monsters" — a leopard girl and a giant "ox-eyed
queen" — the little woman at his elbow asks him to procure her a
chair that she too may see the spectacle. When the giant Queen of
Love calls for a volunteer from the audience to verify that "All
here is honest beauty, flesh and blood", the delighted crowd,
egged on by the little woman's pointing, shouts for her youthful
companion to go up and feel the monster's thigh. Consumed with
rage and embarrassment, the youth approaches, timidly feels the

flesh above the Queen's knee, and flees into the night.

The third section (Sonnets XXI-XXX) is a flashback to the narrator's youth. This section is skillfully placed: having told of his embarrassing retreat, the narrator sets about recalling why he was then such a shy, blushing, unhappy young man. His father, it seems, had met some kind of "tragedy and death on that dark hill" and had become for the family a holy martyr. The youth had subsequently been sheltered from the world by his mother and by his strict, narrow education in the Catholic schools of Rome. Just before coming to Lyons, he had passed the summer "High in the Alps" climbing peaks "with heel fast set / On Nature's neck". Amidst this grandeur he had begun to feel the phantom of his adolescent fears recede: "I seemed to stand, I, too, a man with men".

In the fourth section (Sonnets XXI-XLII) the youth returns, after wandering through the city streets, to the fair — the scene of his recent embarrassment. "The booths were shut". Not far away as he stops before an empty theater to read the handbills about Manon Lescaut played by "Mademoiselle Esther, Muse of Melancholy", a side door opens and out steps the little woman of the fair. She is Mlle. Esther, and she is now delighted to believe that she is pursued by "l'ingénu". She chatters away excitedly about their both being strangers "Among these heavy Lyonnese" and asks, "Would you like we should be friends for good?" The youth is again embarrassed in this new world of the machinations of women: "Not knowing what I said, I said I would". And together they wander through the streets to Esther's dressmaker.

The fifth section (Sonnets XLIII-LI) describes the house of Madame Blanche, the dressmaker, "a certain house still stirring with lights set, / And just a chink left open of the door". Madam Blanche is "a good soul" and does not mind her customers' coming even "At any hour of the night". Amid this woman's world of mirrors and bolts of cloth the youth with his "John the Baptist face" turns "red with confusion", especially when Esther starts removing her clothes and calling, "Bring me the body".

> When Madame Blanche returned to us again
> I was kneeling there, while Esther kissed my face
> And dried and comforted my tears . . .

Having known not only the symbolic "body" of the dressmaker's dummy but also the real fleshly body of Esther, the youthful I has become deified by knowledge. He is now "with Esther the world's gods among", when a few hours before (in Sonnet VI) he "was a stranger a strange world among".

The sixth and concluding section (Sonnets LII-LVIII) recounts the youth's subsequent three days with Esther, "If days be counted by the fall of night / And the sun's rising". While Esther plays her three-day run of Manon, her youthful admirer spends his "term of Glory" as her most ardent backstage Des Grieux. This final section is less particularized by details than the other sections, for it leads immediately into the "surprise" yet inevitable ending of this affair

> When passion prayed its last, and only shame
>   Stood for my portion in a world grown wise,
> And I went forth for ever from her sight
>   Knowing the good and evil. On that day
> I did her wrong by anger. Now life's light
>   Illumines all, and I behold her gay
> As I first knew her in my love purblind,
> Dear passionate Esther, soulless but how kind!

By constructing the poem around three well-drawn scenes (the Lyons fair, the streets outside the theater, Madame Blanche's house) and by the use of dialogue, a consistent point of view of narration, an in medias res beginning, and the flashback technique, Blunt has succeeded in producing the effect of narration that leaves no doubt about character, scene, and event. Yet the integrity of the individual sonnet is maintained. All but five of the sonnets (I, II, III, IV, and XLII) are Shakespearean in metrical pattern, and these five with interlocked octave rimes (abab bcbcdedeff) have functions in indicating the ordering of the story: they mark the four introductory stanzas, and Sonnet XLII marks the climax of the poem. It stands just before the final scene at "Madam Blanche's" and brings to a close the narrator's second meeting with Esther. At this pivotal shift before the denouement — "How shall I tell my fall?" — the rime pattern, echoed from the introductory sonnets, forewarns the ear. In no other sequence does Blunt use his prosody with such telling effect upon the organic unity of the poem. In Esther Blunt wrote his masterpiece.

Natalia's Resurrection, however, which is also in the narrative pattern of the amatory tradition, is not a success. Reminiscent of Boccaccio, Shakespeare, and Tennyson's early long

146

poem, "The Lover's Tale", Blunt's sequence concerns Natalia, who was "wed in youth to one she might not love". Though she still loves Adrian, Natalia as a proud Roman matron will not yield to his pleas of love; instead she feeds him procrastinating promises. When Adrian learns that she is to bear her husband's child, he leaves Rome. Meanwhile Natalia, having "wept dry the fountains of her eyes in grief", has borne her "unliving child and died". When Adrian hears of her death, he makes a three-day ride to Rome. Utterly exhausted upon his arrival, he lies down beneath a cypress tree outside the city walls to rest. He dreams that he is somehow welcomed back to Rome by all his friends, including Natalia's husband. Natalia herself steps forward to tell him "How all was ended now of her old life . . . no longer wife." Together Adrian and his new bride lead all the company to a solemn wedding feast. But the nuptial music blends into the "Miserere Mei Domine" of reality, as Adrian awakes in time to view Natalia's funeral procession. He remains darkly hidden under the cypress trees till nightfall, when among the tombs he finds pick and spade cast down by accident. He digs up Natalia's coffin, and "miracle in sooth renowned above / All wonders of miraculous love!" she lives. "She wakes, she breathes, she rises from her bed", and like Milton's Adam and Eve the lovers depart "Through the dark church with faltering steps and slow".

All of this is a heavy burden of narrative for only thirty-one sonnets. Blunt believed in miracles after his touching Cardinal Newman's hand supposedly cured permanently his toothache, but the narrative line demonstrates his belief that "the soul dies together with the body" and again emphasizes his favorite theme: the power of human love and the joy of its fulfillment. Aside from the narrative, however, there is little else in this sequence. Because of the ill-defined point of view, the remote third-person perspective tends to reduce the sonnets to mere stanzas like Swinburne's use of them in parts of the drama Locrine. The Romeo-Juliet story, which is almost trite and over-coincidental in its juxtaposition of events, does not lend itself to the form of the sonnet sequence. At least, contrasted with Blunt's usual style of impassioned forthrightness, these sonnets, which attempt to suggest the effect of ballad and legend, become flat and dull. An example will illustrate:

XXI [NATALIA'S RESURRECTION]

But when they had gone past him every one,
With new resolve begotten of his dream,
Adrian arose and followed where the stone
Yawned for his love, and there unseen by them
In the dark chauntry he beheld them lay
Her body in the grave with his own heart.
A bitter jest it seemed to him that they
Should all stand near and only he apart,
And through his soul a wind of anger swept
When any in the sad crowd chanced to be
Betwixt him and the woman he so wept,
And oftentimes he cursed them bitterly
That hands not his should touch her in the tomb,
Waiting till night and his revenge should come.

Aside from its metrical pattern, which is constant for the entire
sequence, these lines have little that is characteristic of the
sonnet. The only interesting prosodic detail is the comma at the
end of Sonnet XII, which bridges the merging effect of Adrian's
beginning dream. Natalia's Resurrection demonstrates how
easily the sonnet can become a commonplace stanza and how
ineffective the sonnet sequence can become when it is solely a
narrative vehicle. (10)

(C)

The descriptive-meditative tradition of the sonnet sequence was
developed largely by Wordsworth(11) under the influence of the
single sonnets of Milton and of a few eighteenth-century sonneteers. His The River Duddon, Ecclesiastical Sketches, Poems
Composed or Suggested during a Tour in the Summer of 1833,
Sonnets upon the Punishment of Death, and Personal Talk are
archetypes of this genre. Blunt's three sequences in his tradition — In Vinculis (1889), The Idler's Calendar (1889)(12), and
A New Pilgrimage (1889) — are as a whole less distinguished
than those in the amatory tradition, but written in the years
between Proteus and Esther they indicate Blunt's continued
interest in the sequence as a medium for varied subject matter
and his increasing technical concern with the problems of organic

unity in a poem of poems. In Vinculis: Sonnets Written in an
Irish Prison, 1888, is the least successful of the three; the
work promises more than it fulfills. Its sonnets lack clear chronology or evolution of thought and feeling. The events and his
emotions connected with his Irish imprisonment Blunt handled
later and more effectively in The Land War in Ireland (1912).
The individual titles that were added for the 1914 edition serve
to point up the integrity of the individual sonnets as well as to
imply an underlying narrative thread: "Condemned", "At the
Gate", "Farewell Dark Gaol", "I Will Smile No More". These
four are the titles of the first two and the last two sonnets; they
seem to indicate that the speaker is condemned, that he enters
prison, leaving the world behind him at the gate, and that he is
finally released an embittered man. The sixteen sonnets are
further unified by their Italian metrical patterns, each with fourteen lines employing two or three rime sounds in the octave and
in the sestet. The eight-weeks prison experience was real enough,
but the verse is in the image of a Byron who was momentarily
himself under the influence of Wordsworth. Like the prisoner of
Chillon, Blunt in his Galway Gaol found pleasant distraction in
the living creatures of his cell:

> A spider too for me has spun her thread
> Across the prison rules, and a brave mouse
> Watches in sympathy the warder's tread,
> These two my fellow-prisoners in the house.

The Idler's Calendar, which is Protean in mood, tone, and time
of composition, is neatly unified by its calendrical device of recounting the Idler's pleasures for each of the twelve months:
"January: Cover Shooting", "March: a Week at Paris", "October:
Gambling at Monaco", "December: Away to Egypt". Each of the
twelve sonnets is a caudal sonnet having sixteen lines. "April:
Trout-fishing", for example, concludes:

> Upon the grass he lies, and gasps for air,
> Four silver pounds sublimely fat and fair.

The sequence is further unified by a bantering atmosphere of
pleasure for pleasure's sake. The method is simple, good-
natured description; the total effect is that of vers de société.
The octave of "June: A Day at Hampton Court" illustrates the

ease with which a sonnet sequence can convey the clear charm
of what Professor Tillyard calls "the poetry of statement":

> It is our custom, once in every year,
>> Mine and two others, when the chestnut trees
> Are white at Bushey, Ascot being near,
>> To drive to Hampton Court, and there, at ease
> In that most fair of English palaces,
> Spend a long summer's day. What better cheer
>> Than the old "Greyhounds' ", seek it where you please?
> And where a royal garden statelier?

A New Pilgrimage is more ambitious than either of the two preceding sequences. Its general plan is that of the Wordsworthian
tour. Instead of Yarrow Revisited, here is the Grand Tour revisited. The first five sonnets form an introduction. The pilgrim
would be

> Homeless once more, a wanderer on the earth,
> Marked with my soul's care for company,
>> Like Cain, lest I do murder on my hearth.

And like Childe Harold, he puts his cares and pride behind him
along with his "griefs fog-bound of Father Thames". The method
of unifying these five sonnets is that each raises a question when
the sonnet is read separately that is answered as it progresses.
But when the sonnet is read in sequence, what would be a question
is merely a connective link. For example, Sonnet IV begins,
"Behold the deed is done". The reader who has not read Sonnet III
asks, "What deed?" As he reads on, however, he discovers that
the pilgrim has departed as from a funeral,

> From my dead home, and in the great world's gaze
> Henceforth I stand, a pilgrim of new days,
> On the high road of life.

But for the reader of Sonnet III there is no question; "the deed"
is obviously the Byronic gesture by which the pilgrim would
"break through my bondage. Let me be / Homeless once more".
  In the section on Paris (VI-XX) this same method of linking the
sonnets in series can be illustrated on the simpler level of demonstrative pronouns and adjectives. In Sonnet XI "these flowers"

points backward to the blue gentians of Sonnet X and forward to the phrase "Treasures we gathered there, long sere and brown". The opening words of Sonnet XV, "For thus it is", point backward to the idea of the fast-shifting governments of France and forward to

> You flout at kings to-day.
> Tomorrow in your pride you shall stoop low
> To a new tyrant.

Thus the individual sonnet is understandable in its own right yet firmly joined to its predecessors.

Like Meredith, Blunt achieves the effect of narration by the flashback technique. Instead of pausing in his travels for a diorama of local history as Childe Harold does, the new pilgrim pauses to recall scenes of former visits: travels through the chestnut woods of Bearn and through the ancient cities of Havre and Caen when as children Wilfrid, Francis, and Alice had ridden in the old family coach with their mother. The Paris of Wilfrid's days as attaché are also recalled when "Later, I too my love diplomacies / Played at Eugenia's court".

The design of the third section (XXI-XXIX) is similar but in inverted proportion: instead of the one-third in the former section two-thirds are devoted to memories of living in "the land of lakes and snow". In Sonnet XXX Moses-like the new pilgrim "stepped from Horeb to the plains" of northern Italy. The last eleven sonnets (XXX-XL) concern Italy—not the political state whose struggles had inspired the Brownings and Swinburne, but the Italy of the Catholic Church. Blunt kneels "at last . . . in Rome", sees Pope Leo "sitting on a kingly throne, / A man of age, whom Time had touched with white". But the end of this "sad soul's pilgrimage" is regret. For this latter-day Childe Harold in "the clamour of vain days" Rome's mission can be only

> To guard the calm of Man's birth
> And like an eagle to renew his days.

The individual sonnets of <u>A New Pilgrimage</u> all contain fourteen lines with the thought division usually following the octave-sestet pattern. All end with couplets, and the rimes are more exact with fewer experiments in assonance. (13) His growing concern

with metrical similarity of individual sonnets, experimentation
in the flashback technique, and occasional dialogue show Blunt's
developing interest in a skillfully ordered method of sonnet narration that found its best expression in Esther.

Though Blunt's style and even his phraseology are occasionally reminiscent in turn of Shakespeare, Milton, Byron, Keats,
Tennyson, Browning, or Owen Meredith, his work in the architectonics of the sonnet sequence shows originality. Blunt began
his sonnet career by putting together a little volume of verse
and prose in 1867. Believing that only the sonnets were not
"worthless", he next compiled the volume entitled Sonnets and
Songs by Proteus (1881), the sonnets of which went through
varying stages of additions and deletions until its final version
in 1914. The long experimentation with devices for unifying a
poem in sonnets, as is demonstrated in the various editions of
Proteus, and the slow development of the narrative method that
evolved from the "Farewell to Juliet" section of Proteus through
the flashback sections of A New Pilgrimage help to explain the
originality and effectiveness of Esther. Although the latter poem
is sometimes judged as derivative in technique from Modern
Love, there is external evidence for believing that Blunt had not
read that poem when he wrote Esther, (14) and there is also little
convincing internal evidence of similarity or influence. At least,
in subject matter and in method of narration Esther is the logical culmination of Blunt's own interests, backgrounds, and poetic
techniques.

(D)

To appreciate the significance of Blunt's special contribution to
the genre of the sonnet sequence, it is necessary to consider his
sonnets against the background of a raison d'être for that form.
For every genre in every art form there is a central median or
norm that makes that form recognizable and the treatment of its
subject matter unique. This median is usually somewhat elastic
and may be stretched in many directions to achieve different
patterns and thereby that shade of variety and uniqueness necessary for any great work of art. If the process of stretching, however, exceeds a certain, if variously defined, norm, the resulting
"pattern" becomes either chaotic or too similar to the median of
some other genre. Shakespeare's sonnets and Mrs. Browning's

Sonnets from the Portuguese have established for the amatory
tradition a kind of norm wherein the sonnets remain individual
poems, while suggesting a love story by implication. Rossetti
has stretched this median in one direction and Meredith in another, and each has achieved a valid work of art. The House of
Life, the Victorian archetype of the amatory-lyric tradition, is
musically unified by the tone and mood of its individual sonnets
and by intricate weavings on themes of love, life, and death;
but there is no implied story. Modern Love, on the other hand,
suggests a norm for a new pattern for the amatory-narrative
tradition by its complicated and subtle story with the individual
sonnets each reflecting some aspect of that story.

Blunt's Love Sonnets of Proteus remains close to the norm of
the amatory tradition: it unfolds by implication; its merit lies
more in its individual sonnets than in the whole work. Its special
contribution is the variety of means by which its four parts
maintain a certain surface unity. "Gods and False Gods", for
example, is loose in its weaving of themes like The House of
Life, the "Farewell to Juliet" sonnets are close to the narrative
technique of Modern Love, and "To Manon" is written in the
median tradition of Sonnets from the Portuguese.

In Esther Blunt has stretched the norm beyond the point of
Modern Love and in a slightly different direction. Instead of implying or even reflecting episodes of a story, he employs individual sonnets to create the complete details of fully drawn
scenes, and at strategic intervals, other sonnets to meditate
and philosophize briefly upon these scenes. The sonnets thus
maintain a delicate balance between the individual integrity of
a lyric medium and the stanzaic unity of a narrative medium.
Esther suggests the total effect of fiction without itself becoming
entirely narrative. This is the raison d'être for the sonnet sequence: the power to suggest the effects of other verse media
without becoming in turn those media themselves and without
sacrificing the principal hallmarks of sonnet structure. This
quality in Esther makes it Blunt's most original contribution to
the genre of the sonnet sequence. In Natalia's Resurrection,
however, the norm has been stretched too far, and the resulting
poem no longer implies the medium of the legend - it actually
becomes a Roman legend of love told in fourteen-line stanzas.
The integrity of the individual poems is swallowed up in the
whole, and the peculiar blend of meditative and lyric qualities
that characterize the sonnet is lost in the narration of events.

It is undoubtedly true that in superficial as well as in detailed critical judgments of sonnet sequences a double standard of values must be employed: the merits of the individual sonnets as poems must be weighted against the merits of the whole poem. That there must be a unity within a unity makes the genre a complicated one to create or evaluate. The challenge of its composition has attracted poetasters like Martin Tupper and Ebenezer Elliott, who were concerned chiefly with its external intricacies, (15) and major poets like Sidney, Shakespeare, Wordsworth, Rossetti, and Meredith, who were alive to the total implications of the genre.

In 1913 when Blunt was arranging the final edition of his poetry, he had not written a sonnet sequence for over twenty years. Looking back at his six sequences, he apparently attempted to indicate their differences, and at the same time by clarifying subtitles and individual sonnet titles he hinted something of his conception of the term "sonnet sequence", a Victorian term first used by Rossetti (then by Swinburne, Symonds, William Sharp, and others) and employed by Victorian and modern critics to refer to all sonnet groupings. With none of his sequences had he employed the term "sonnet sequence" before Poetical Works (1914). In the preface to A New Pilgrimage Blunt refers to that poem as a "series". The Love Sonnets of Proteus he left in the final arrangement with no subtitle and with the individual sonnets entitled separately or in groups. To In Vinculis he added individual titles to the sixteen sonnets, and to The Idler's Calendar he added the subtitle Twelve Sonnets for the Months, retaining the individual headings for each sonnet. To A New Pilgrimage, Esther, and Natalia's Resurrection he added the term "Sonnet Sequence", from which he omitted the hyphen that Rossetti, Swinburne, Watts-Dunton, and others had used before him. Furthermore, none of these three sequences has separately titled individual sonnets; in each case they are merely numbered. It seems evident, then, that so far as his own poetry was concerned Blunt would reserve the term "sonnet sequence" for those groups of sonnets closely unified in style and content, where the individual sonnets have taken on some of the characteristics of stanzas and where the majority cannot be transposed at will even though individual sonnet integrity is maintained. By adding the subtitle "Sonnet Sequence" to his last three and not to his first three poems in this genre Blunt further indicates that for him the term contains narrative implications.

For some of his contemporaries Wilfrid Scawen Blunt had
the glamorous reputation of world traveler, defender of the
rights of oppressed peoples, and squire and horse breeder of
Crabbet Park. For others he was anathema: they would have
agreed with the Prince of Wales that Blunt was a "disloyal and
eccentric Jesuit" bent on undermining the British Empire. (16)
But to a younger generation the man, if not the poet, became
a symbol for a new century of human rights as Pound sees him
in the Pisan Cantos:

> But to have done instead of not doing
>   this is not vanity
> To have, with decency, knocked
> That a Blunt should open
>   To have gathered from the air a live tradition
> or from a fine old eye the unconquered flame
> This is not vanity.

For present-day readers Blunt has become a well-informed
chronicler of his times—a reputation that will grow when the
full extent of his manuscript "Histories" can be published—
and a minor late-Victorian poet "a little in advance of his
epoch". To Blunt's present reputation should be added the fact
that during the last two decades of the nineteenth century his
sonnet sequences summarized the main traditions of the genre
and indicated new ways of handling narrative in this basically
lyric medium.

NOTES

(1) Biographical facts about Blunt can best be found in his auto-
biographical writings, My Diaries (New York: Knopf, 1922),
Ideas about India (London: Kegan Paul, 1885), The Land War in
Ireland (London: Stephen Swift, 1912), for example; in Edith
Finch, Wilfrid Scawen Blunt, 1840-1922 (London: Jonathan Cape,
1938), The [Fourth] Earl of Lytton, Wilfrid Scawen Blunt, A
Memoir by His Grandson (London: Macdonald, 1961), and in
reminiscences of friends and acquaintances like Frank Harris,
Lady Gregory, Siegfried Sassoon, Samuel C. Chew, T. P.
O'Connor, Esme Howard, The First Earl of Lytton, Lady

Lutyens, et al. In addition to the Diaries and the six volumes
of the Secret History Series, there is a quantity of manuscript
material, upon which some of these works are based, now
housed in the Fitzwilliam Museum at Cambridge. Mr. Carl
Winter, director of the museum in 1953, explained to me that
the Blunt papers "were opened September last, in accordance
with instructions left by him. After examination by the Syndics
and their expert advisers the Syndicate decided that so much
of the material in the boxes is unsuitable for publication at the
present time that the task of separating what could not be published from what could not would be so exacting that they must
re-seal the boxes for a further period of twenty years. This is
in accordance with Blunt's original proposal suggesting that the
papers be kept unopened for fifty years after his death, which
he subsequently modified to allow the Syndicate to consider the
matter after thirty years."
(2) Lady Gregory in her preface to Blunt's Diaries states that
he was "the first Englishman put in prison for Ireland's sake".
(3) E. M. Foster, Abinger Harvest (New York: Harcourt, 1936),
p. 238.
(4) William Butler Yeats wrote the account of this occasion for
the London Times, June 20, 1914, p. 5; see also Finch, pp.
336-338, and my "A Peacock Dinner: The Homage of Pound and
Yeats to Wilfrid Scawen Blunt", Journal of Modern Literature,
1 (1971) 303-310.
(5) The Copeland and Day (Boston) edition of 1895 adds a sonnet, "To Griselda: A Letter", from Griselda: A Society Novel
in Rhymed Verse (1893), bringing the total to 142. It is doubtful that Blunt authorized this addition.
(6) One of the best accounts of Skittles can be found in William
Hardman, A Mid-Victorian Pepys: The Letters and Memoirs,
annotated and edited by S. M. Ellis (London: Cecil Palmer, 1924),
pp. 210-216. See also my "Blunt's Sonnets and Skittles: A
Further Word", VP, 4 (1966) 137-141.
(7) The majority of the sonnets contain fourteen lines though
both Blunt and Symonds, like the early Italian poets, occasionally employed the extended sonnet form.
(8) Mr. Winter of the Fitzwilliam Museum states: "The blank
verse version of Esther, consisting of ten sheets of manuscript,
is included in the papers of Blunt's White Deed Box, in an en-
velope inscribed 'First sketch of Esther — as sent to Robert
Lytton in 1866'."

(9) The texts of these sonnets as well as that of all of Blunt's quoted poetry is from Poetical Works, 2 vols. (London: Macmillan, 1914).

(10) Perhaps the closest analogue for Natalia's Resurrection is Robert Stephen Hawker's "Annot of Benallay", which first appeared in Records of the Western Shore in 1832.

(11) Wordsworth's term for this category would have been "locodescriptive"—the classification he used in the 1815 edition of his poems (see the first essay in this volume).

(12) In the preface to A New Pilgrimage and Other Poems Blunt intimates, however, that The Idler's Calendar belongs "to the author's period of 'Proteus'."

(13) The preface to A New Pilgrimage also defends Blunt's theories of sonnet structure as well as his preference for assonance, which he learned to like from his study of Arabic.

(14) When Esther appeared in 1892, Meredith wrote Blunt "a letter of high approval, sending him 'Modern Love', which was even then unknown to him" (Siegfried Sassoon, Meredith [New York: Viking, 1948], p. 226). When I asked his authority for this statement Mr. Sassoon replied that this was the uncompromising opinion of Sir Sidney Cockerell, Blunt's former part-time secretary. By 1893, however, Blunt was quoting an epigraph from Modern Love for his verse novel, Griselda.

(15) "As to the poetical part, objections may be urged against the exclusive adoption of the sonnet, in preference to the varieties of lyric composition: but the writer has aimed at uniformity, and has selected that mode which he hoped was the most classical, although he has felt it greatly the most difficult" (Martin Tupper, A Modern Pyramid: To Commemorate a Septuagint of Worthies [London: Joseph Rickerly, 1839], preface, p. xi).

(16) Sir Sidney Lee, King Edward VII, A Biography (London: Macmillan, 1935), I, 458.

APPENDIX

A REPRESENTATIVE LIST OF BRITISH SONNET SEQUENCES
OF THE EIGHTEENTH AND NINETEENTH CENTURIES

This list of some 260 sequences, containing almost 4800 sonnets,
is intended merely to be representative of the wide interest in
sonnet groupings that began its revival in the closing decades of
the eighteenth century and has continued to the present time.
Major poets, minor poets, and poetasters have found the form
useful — indeed no other single lyric form has appealed to so
many poets in so many Western languages over so long a period
of time.

For the purposes of this list of late-eighteenth and nineteenth-
century British sequences, the sequence itself is defined as
three or more sonnets arranged by the author or his "official"
editor under a single title and/or planned to be read chronologically. The dates, unless otherwise noted, are those of first
major publication (usually in book form), so far as I have been
able to verify them. The numbers in parentheses indicate the
number of sonnets in each sequence. Often that number varies
from edition to edition, and for a few of the more significant
sequences I have indicated the variation. Occasionally the number depends upon whether introductory and dedicatory sonnets
are to be counted and upon other exigencies of printing.

I have found helpful the anthologies of sonnets of the nineteenth
century, especially William Sharp, ed., Sonnets of This [Nine-
teenth] Century (London: Walter Scott, [1886]); R.D. Havens,
The Influence of Milton on English Poetry (Cambridge, Mass.:
Harvard Univ. Press, 1922), and "More Eighteenth-Century
Sonnets", MLN, 45 (1930), 77-84; Paul Everett Reynolds, The
English Sonnet Sequence, 1784-1845 (Unpublished Harvard dis-
sertation, 1938) [a study of fourteen sequences]; George Sanderlin,
"The Influence of Milton and Wordsworth on the Early Victorian
Sonnet", ELH, 5(1938) 225-251, and The Sonnet in English
Literature 1800-1850 (Unpublished John Hopkins dissertation,
1938); Houston Peterson, ed., The Book of Sonnet Sequences
(New York: Longmans, 1930); Bruce B. Clark, The English Son-
net Sequence, 1850-1900: A Study of Fourteen Sequences (Unpub-
lished Univ. of Utah dissertation, 1951); and the library shelves
of Duke, Michigan, Columbia, Harvard, Washington, and Southern
Illinois universities.

1781   Charles Emily, Death (18)
1783   Edmund Cartwright [?], Sonnets to Eminent Men (6)
1787   'Benedict', [Ten Sonnets Addressed to 'Melissa'] (10)(n1)
1793   Alexander Thomson, Six Sonnets from "Werter" (6)
1794-95 Samuel Taylor Coleridge, Sonnets on Eminent Charac-
            ters (14)
1796   -   , Sonnet[s] on Receiving a Letter Informing Me of
            the Birth of a Son (3)(n2)
1796   Mrs. Mary Robinson, Sappho and Phaon, in a Series of
            Legitimate Sonnets. . . (44)
1796-97 Charles Lamb, "Was it some sweet Device of Faery"
            [Sonnets to Ann Simmons] (6)
1797   Charles Lloyd, Poems, on the Death of Priscilla
            Farmer, by her Grandson (10)
1797   Robert Southey, Poems on the Slave Trade (6) (n3)
1797   Samuel Taylor Coleridge, Sonnets Attempted in the
            Manner of Contemporary Writers (3)
1800   Ann Bannerman, Sonnets from "Werter" (10)
1807   -   , Sonnets from Petrarch (4)
1807   William Wordsworth, Personal Talk (4)
          -   , To Sleep (3) (n4)
1808   John Henry Kenney, Sonnets to the Memory of a Beloved
            Object (7)
1814   Capel Lofft, La Corona. The Wreath (15)(n5)
1815   Leigh Hunt, To Hampstead (5)
1817   John Keats, "Woman! when I behold thee flippant, vain"
            (3)
1818   Leigh Hunt, To -, M.D.: on his Giving Me a Lock of
            Milton's Hair (3)
1819   Samuel Egerton Brydges, Five Sonnets Addressed to
            Wooton, the Spot of the Author's Nativity (5)
1820   William Wordsworth, The River Duddon, A Series of
            Sonnets (34)
1820   Barry Cornwall, Sonnets: Spring, Summer, Autumn,
            Winter (4)
1820   William Curtis, Amoretti (30)
1821   Thomas Lovell Beddoes, Quatorzains (13)
1822   William Wordsworth, Ecclesiastical Sketches (102 in
            1822; 132 in 1845; called Ecclesiastical Sonnets:
            In Series after 1835)

1827 Charles Strong, <u>Specimens of Sonnets from the most</u>
     <u>celebrated Italian Poets with Translations</u>
     [Italian and English on facing pages, from
     Dante to Metastasio] (50)

1828-29 Isaac Williams, <u>The Golden Valley</u> (63)
   - , <u>The Country Pastor</u> (41)

1830 Alfred Tennyson, <u>Love</u> (3)

1830 Arthur Hallam, [<u>Seven Italian Sonnets</u>] (7)

1831 - , <u>Sonnets Written after My Return from Somersby</u>
     (9) (n6)

1832 - , <u>Translations from the "Vita Nuova" of Dante</u> (25)
     (n7)

1833 Hartley Coleridge, <u>To a Friend</u> (3)

1834 Arthur Hallam, ["Somersby Sonnets"] (9) (n8)

1834 Thomas Pringle, <u>Sonnets</u> [in <u>African Sketches</u>] (14)

1834 Richard Monckton Milnes, <u>The Illumination of St.</u>
     <u>Peters</u> (3)

1834 Mrs. Felicia Hemans, <u>Sonnets, Devotional and Mem-</u>
     <u>orial</u> (17)
   - , <u>Female Characters of Scripture</u> (15)

1835 John Clare, <u>The Lout</u> (3)

1835 James Montgomery, <u>A Sea-Piece: In Three Sonnets</u> (3)

1835 William Wordsworth, <u>Poems Composed or Suggested</u>
     <u>during a Tour in the Summer of 1833</u> (45)
   - , <u>Yarrow Revisited</u> (23)

1836 Samuel Egerton Brydges, <u>Hastings' Sonnets</u> (8)

1836 Mrs. Felicia Hemans, <u>Records of the Spring of 1834</u> (21)
   - , <u>Records of the Autumn of 1834</u> (10)

1837 Samuel Egerton Brydges, <u>Three Sonnets to Jean Müller,</u>
     <u>the Historian</u> (3)
   - , <u>Sonnets, Written in the Character of Tasso</u> (11)
   - , <u>Prince Henry to the Countess of Essex</u> (6) (other
     groupings among 2200 sonnets in manuscript left
     to the British Museum and the London Library,
     including a narrative one, "Alda Norwood" [53])

1837 E. M. H[amilton], <u>Sonnets: Suggested by revisiting (in</u>
     <u>August, 1837, after an Absence from Ireland)</u>
     <u>Glendalough and Other Parts</u> of the County
     Wicklow (5) (n9)

1837 Benmajin Disraeli, [Sonnet Sequence in <u>Venetia</u>] (11)

1837 Iota, <u>Music: Three Sonnets by Iota</u> (3)(n10)

1837 J. U. U., <u>Westminster Abbey</u> (8)(n11)

1838	Thomas Burbidge, <u>Spring Sonnets</u> (15)
1839	Martin Tupper, <u>A Modern Pyramid: To Commemorate a Septuagint of Worthies</u> (70)
1839	Mrs. Felicia Hemans, <u>Thoughts during Sickness</u> (7)
1840	Richard Monckton Milnes, <u>On the Church of the Madeleine at Paris</u> (3)
1840	Ebenezer Elliott, <u>Rhymed Rambles</u> (47)
1840	Frederick William Faber, <u>Memorials of a Happy Time</u> (20)
-	, <u>The Four Religious Heathen</u> (4)
1841	Henry Alford, <u>Pictorial Emblems for the Seasons</u> (4)
1841	William Wordsworth, <u>Sonnets upon the Punishment of Death</u> (14)
1842	- , <u>Memorials of a Tour in Italy, 1837</u> (23)
-	, <u>The Widow on Windermere Side</u> (3)
-	, <u>In Allusion to Various Recent Histories and Notices of the French Revolution</u> (3)(n12)
1842	Sir Aubrey de Vere, <u>Prayer</u> (3)
-	, <u>Atlantic Coast Scenery</u> (9)
-	, <u>The Crusaders</u> (8)
-	, <u>Columbus</u> (3)
-	, <u>On the Lord's Prayer</u> (23) (among 152 sonnets divided into five groups)
1843	David Macbeth Moir, <u>Sonnets on the Scenery of the Tweed</u> (7)
1843	Isaac Williams, <u>The Cloisters: Ecclesiastical Sonnets</u> (28)
1844	Leigh Hunt, <u>The Fish, the Man, and the Spirit</u> (3)
-	, <u>To the Author of "Ion"</u> (3)
1844-45	Anonymous, <u>A Rosary from the Rhine</u> (78)(n13)
1845	William Wordsworth, <u>Sonnets Dedicated to Liberty and Order</u> (14)
1846	'A Young Englander', <u>Thirty-Six Nonconformist Sonnets</u> (36)(n14)
1846	Martin Tupper, <u>Contrasted Sonnets</u> (30)
1847	Isaac Williams, <u>The Altar</u> (204) (other religious groupings among 374 sonnets)
1847	Robert Ferguson, <u>The Shadow of the Pyramid: A Series of Sonnets</u> (68)
1849	Arthur Hugh Clough, <u>Commemoration Sonnets: Oxford, 1844</u> (3)
1849	Dante Gabriel Rossetti, <u>Last Sonnets at Paris</u> (3)(n15)

1850	Dante Gabriel Rossetti, Sonnets for Pictures (6) (n16)
1850	Elizabeth Barret Browning, Sonnets from the Portuguese (43) (44 in 1856)
-	, Hugh Stuart Boyd (3)
1851	George Meredith, Pictures of the Rhine (6)
1851	Richard C. Trench, Vesuvius (3)
-	, To a Lady Singing (6)
1851	Hartley Coleridge, [To William Wordsworth] (17)
-	, [Sonnets Suggested by the Seasons] (17)
-	, To an Infant (3)
1851	- , [Sonnets . . . on Scriptural and Religious Subjects] (33) (These groupings are mainly the editing of Derwent Coleridge.)
1852	David Macbeth Moir, Sonnets on the Scenery of the Esk (6)
-	, Winter (5)
-	, The Scottish Sabbath (6)
1854	Catherine Godwin, Four Sonnets Written during a Summer Tour on the Continent (4)
1855	Alexander Smith and The Author of "Balder" and "The Roman" [Sidney Dobell], Sonnets on the War (39)
1855	Aubrey Thomas de Vere, Sonnets Written in Travel (43) (Many of these sonnets were called Sonnets Chiefly on Medieval Art in 1893.)
-	, [Irish] Colonization, 1848 (5)
1857	George MacDonald, Four Sonnets: Inscribed to S.F.S., because the second is about her father (4)
-	, Eighteen Sonnets, About Jesus (18) (called Concerning Jesus, 1893)
1857	John Stuart Blackie, Highland Sonnets (9)
-	, German Sonnets (8)
1857	Frederick William Faber, The Old French Telegraphs (4)
-	, Thoughts While Reading History (20)
1857	Algernon Charles Swinburne, Undergraduate Sonnets (7) (n17)
1859	Richard Garnett, Sonnets from Mickiewicz [translations] (4)
1861	Dante Gabriel Rossetti, The Early Italian Poets [translations including, among 174 sonnets, 35 from Dante's Vita Nuova]
1862	David Gray, In the Shadows (30)
1862	George Meredith, Modern Love (50)

1864   Charles Tennyson Turner, Great Localities: An Inspi-
          ration (3)
      –   , Hebron (3)
      –   , Christ and Orpheus (3) (Many pairs and some
          longer groups are evident, though not so indi-
          cated, among the 342 sonnets of Collected Son-
          nets [1880].)
1865   Alfred Tennyson, Three Sonnets to a Coquette (3)
1865   Gerard Manley Hopkins, The Beginning of the End (3) (n18)
1866   Algernon Charles Swinburne, Hermaphroditus (4)
1867   Matthew Arnold, Rachel (3)
1869   Aubrey Thomas de Vere, Urbs Roma (27) (other religious
          groupings among 324 sonnets often re-grouped
          from edition to edition)
1869   Arthur Hugh Clough, Seven Sonnets [on the Thought of
          Death] (7)
1870   John Charles Earle, A Hundred Sonnets (100) (Many
          loosely arranged groupings here and in Second
          Hundred Sonnets [1871] and in Light Leading un-
          to Light [1875].)
1870   Dante Gabriel Rossetti, "Sonnets and Songs Toward a
          Work to be called 'The House of Life'" (50)
          (sixteen published in the Fortnightly in 1869;
          101 in 1881 and titled The House of Life: A Son-
          net-Sequence)
1870   Robert Buchanan, Sonnets Written by Loch Coruisk (34)
1871   Philip Bourke Marston, Sonnets (in Song-Tide) (47)
      –   , Across Seas: To Björnsterne Björnson, Author
          of "Arne" (4)
1871   John Payne, Winter Roses (9)
      –   , Madonna Dei Sogni (14)
      –   , On the Borders of the Night (5)
      –   , Azaleas (A Picture by Albert Moore) (3)
1872   Andrew Lang, To Poets (5)
1873   Edmund Gosse, Fortunate Love (20)
1873   Isa Blagden, The Seven Chords of the Lyre (7)
1874   George Eliot, Brother and Sister (11)
1875   Philip Bourke Marston, Preludes (8)
1875   Cora Kennedy Aitken, Sonnets for the People (30)
      –   , Maria Mazzanti to Niccolo Polini, Dead (15)
1875   William Bell Scott, Outside the Temple: Sonnets (16)
      –   , Parted Love (5)
      –   , The Old Scotch House (Penkill Ayrshire) Part I (7)

	– , Sonnets on Literary Subjects [including three on Wordsworth] (11)
1875	Philip Acton, Sonnets on Immortality (14)
1875	Sydney Dobell, To 1862 (5)
	– , Three Sonnets on Love and Beauty (3)
1875	Algernon Charles Swinburne, Dirae (24)
1876	Ebenezer Elliott, The Year of Seeds: 1848 (50)(n19)
1876	Edward Dowden, In the Galleries (5)
	– , In the Garden (8)
	– , By the Sea (7)
	– , Memorials of Travel (9)
	– , The Inner Life (12)
	– , From April to October (11)
1876	Westland Marston, Scenes in Normandy (3)(n20)
1877	Gerard Manley Hopkins, [Ten Sonnets Written in Wales during 1877] (10)(n21)
1877	Aubrey Thomas de Vere, To E. (4)
	– , The Beatific Vision of Earth (3)
	– , In Memory of the Late Sir John Simon (3)
1878	John Addington Symonds, Sonnets on the Thought of Death (22)
	– , The Genius of the Vatican (7)
	– , In Quest Selva Selvaggia (3) (included in The Alps and Italy, 1880)
1878	Richard Wilton, Sonnets on the Fathers (8)
	– , Sonnets on the Types (11)
1880	John Payne, Indian Summer (4)
	– , Les Soirs de Londres [in French] (4)
	– , Sarvarthasiddha-Buddha (4)
1880	John Addington Symonds, Intellectual Isolation (7)
	– , Friendship, Love and Death (3)
	– , In Absence (3)
	– , An Old Gordian Knot (8)
	– , The Alps and Italy (8)
1881	Wilfrid Scawen Blunt, The Love Sonnets of Proteus (106) (141 in 1892; 142 in 1895; 114 in 1914)
1881	Dante Gabriel Rossetti, Five English Poets (5)
1881	Christina Rossetti, Monna Innominata: A Sonnet of Sonnets (14)
	– , Later Life: A Double Sonnet of Sonnets (28)
	– , The Thread of Life (3)
	– , If Thou Sayest, Behold, We Knew It Not (3)

1881   Oscar Wilde, <u>Impressions du Théâtre</u> (5)
1881   H. D. Rawnsley, <u>Sonnets at the English Lakes</u> (121)
1882   Algernon Charles Swinburne, <u>Sonnets of English Dramatic</u>
                <u>Poets</u> (1590-1650) (21)
        -   , <u>After Sunset</u> (3)
1882   Alfred Austin, <u>Three Sonnets Written in Mid-Channel</u> (3)
1882   John Addington Symonds, <u>Animi Figura</u> (140) (divided in-
                to groups; includes those of 1880)
1882   Emily Pfeiffer, <u>A Plea</u> (4)
1883   George MacDonald, <u>My Two Geniuses</u> (3)
1883   Philip Bourke Marston, <u>Sonnets to C. N. M.</u> (6)
        -   , <u>Moments of Vision</u> (3)
        -   , <u>Parables</u> (5)
        -   , <u>Sonnets on Sorrow</u> (3)
        -   , <u>The Temptress</u> (3)
1883   Robert Browning, "<u>Moses the meek</u>" [Jochanan
                Hakkadosh] (3)
1884   William Sharp, <u>Sonnets on Three Paintings by Bazzi</u>
                (Sodoma) (3)
1884   Alexander Winton Buchan, <u>On Reading Shakespeare</u> (3)
        -   , <u>God in All</u> (3)
        -   , <u>By the Sea</u> (4)
        -   , <u>To a Bereaved Pair</u> (3)
1884   Aubrey Thomas de Vere, <u>Memorial Sonnets</u> (3)
        -   , <u>Wordsworth</u> (3)
1884   John Addington Symonds, <u>Stella Maris</u> (67)
        -   , <u>The Sea Calls</u> (6)
        -   , <u>Winter Nights in the High Alps</u> (4)
        -   , <u>In Black and White—Winter Etchings</u> (6)
        -   , <u>The Envoy to a Book</u> (6)
        -   , <u>The Sonnet</u> (3)
        -   , <u>Monte Generoso</u> (3)
        -   , <u>To the Beloved</u> (after Philostratus) (4)
1884   Algernon Charles Swinburne, <u>Pelagius</u> (3)
        -   , <u>Louis Blanc: Three Sonnets to His Memory</u> (3)
        -   , <u>Vos Deos Laudamus</u> (3)
        -   , <u>Love and Scorn</u> (3)
        -   , <u>In Sepulcretis</u> (4)
1885   Gerard Manley Hopkins, [<u>Sonnets of Desolation</u>] (6) (n22)
1885   Roden Noel, <u>Political Sonnets</u> (4)
        -   , <u>The Death of Livingstone</u> (8)
1885   Edward Cracroft Lefroy, <u>Echoes from Theocritus</u> (30)
        -   , <u>A Woodland Stream</u> (5)

1896   William Watson, The Purple East (17)
1896   Fiona Macleod (William Sharp), The Shepherd (3)
1896   Richard Garnett, Dante, Petrarch, Camoens: CXXIV
                      Sonnets [translations] (124)
1897   A.C. Benson, Self (4)
1898   Theodore Watts-Dunton, Four Sonnets to Those Who
                      Carry the Tongue of Shakespeare Round the
                      World (4)
    -    , A Grave by the Sea (5)
    -    , What the Silent Voices Said (6)
    -    , Apollo in Paris (4)
    -    , The Last Walk from Boar's Hill (3)
    -    , Natura Benigna (13) (includes other lyrics)
    -    , The Three Fausts (3)
1898   Thomas Hardy, She, to Him (4)
1898   W.E. Henley, London Types (13)
1898   Robert Louis Stevenson, Brasheanna: Sonnets on Peter
                      Brash, a Publican (5)(n26)
1899   H.D. Rawnsley, Sonnets in Switzerland and Italy (163)
1899   Alfred Douglas, A Triad of the Moon (3)
    -    , The City of the Soul (4)
1904   Algernon Charles Swinburne, Apostasy (4)
1904   Frederic W.H. Myers, A Cosmic Outlook (3) (n27)
1907   William Michael Rossetti, Democratic Sonnets (50)(n28)
1907   Theodore Watts-Dunton, The Rhodes Memorial at
                      Oxford: The Work of Cecil Rhodes; A Sonnet-
                      Sequence (8)
1909   Eugene Lee-Hamilton, Mimma Bella (29)
1909   Alfred Douglas, To Olive (6)
1909   William Watson, Sonnets to Miranda (17)
1913   Arthur Symons, The Brother of a Weed (5)

NOTES

(1) Printed in The World
(2) Date of composition (two were published in 1797, one in
1847).
(3) Never actually titled, but placed in a section, "Poems on
the Slave Trade" (Poems [1797]).
(4) Not so grouped by W.W. except by the same title for each
(composed and published at the same time).

(5) An appendix to <u>Laura, or an Anthology of Sonnets</u> — including 44 by Petrarch with translations.

(6) Date of composition, published posthumously (three 1943, all nine in 1965).

(7) Translated 1827-32, published posthumously in 1943.

(8) Three printed in 1834, three in 1943, and three in 1965.

(9) Printed in the <u>Dublin University Magazine</u>.

(10) Printed in the <u>Dublin University Magazine</u>.

(11) Printed in the <u>Dublin University Magazine</u>.

(12) Included in <u>Sonnets Dedicated to Liberty and Order</u> in 1845.

(13) Printed in <u>Tait's Edinburgh Magazine</u>.

(14) Printed in <u>The Athenaeum</u>.

(15) Date of composition, published posthumously in 1895.

(16) Printed in <u>The Germ</u> (called <u>Art and Poetry</u>, May, 1850); grouping expanded in "Sonnets for Pictures and Other Sonnets" in <u>Poems</u>, 1870; grouping restored and increased to 11 by William Michael Rossetti's editing in <u>Collected Poems</u>, 1886.

(17) Approximate date of composition, published posthumously in 1918.

(18) Date of composition, published posthumously in 1935.

(19) Published posthumously in <u>Poetical Works</u>, ed. by his son.

(20) "Composed some years earlier."

(21) Date of composition, published posthumously in 1918.

(22) Date of composition, published posthumously in 1918.

(23) Approximate date of composition (Sonnet IV was published in 1886, Sonnet VIII in 1896, the entire sequence in 1934).

(24) Approximate date of composition, published posthumously in 1913.

(25) Published posthumously in William Michael Rossetti's edition of her <u>New Poems</u>.

(26) Written in 1881, the first sonnet was published in 1898, the rest privately printed in 1913, and the whole series put with R. L. S. 's collected verse in 1950.

(27) Published posthumously.

(28) Fourteen additional sonnets printed in <u>Victorian Studies</u> (March, 1971).

BIBLIOGRAPHY OF WORKS CITED

Allingham, William, A Diary. Ed. H. Allingham and D. Radford.
     London: Macmillan, 1907.
Anderson, Warren D., Matthew Arnold and the Classical Tra-
     dition. Ann Arbor: Univ. of Mich. Press, 1965.
Arishstein, Leonid M. and William E. Fredeman, "William
     Michael Rossetti's 'Democratic Sonnets' ". Victorian
     Studies, 14 (1971), 241-74.
Arnold, Matthew, Essays in Criticism, Second Series. London:
     Macmillan, 1896.
-     , Essays, Letters and Reviews. Ed. Fraser Neiman.
     Cambridge, Mass.: Harvard Univ. Press, 1960.
-     , Letters, 1848-1888. Ed. G.W.E. Russell. 2 vols.
     London: Macmillan, 1895.
-     , The Letters of Matthew Arnold to Arthur Hugh Clough.
     Ed. H.F. Lowry. London: Oxford Univ. Press, 1932.
-     , The Note-books. Ed. H.F. Foster, Karl Young, and
     W.H. Dunn. London: Oxford Univ. Press, 1952.
-     , The Poems. Ed. Kenneth Allott. New York: Barnes &
     Noble, 1965.
Bartlett, Phyllis, "A Manuscript of Meredith's 'Modern Love' ".
     The Yale University Library Gazette, 40 (1966), 185-87.
Baum, Paull F., Tennyson Sixty Years After. Chapel Hill: Univ.
     of North Carolina Press, 1948.
-     , Ten Studies in the Poetry of Matthew Arnold. Durham,
     N.C.: Duke Univ. Press, 1958.
Blunt, Wilfrid Scawen, My Diaries. 2 vols. New York: Knopf,
     1922.
-     , Ideas About India. London: Kegan Paul, 1885.
-     , The Land War in Ireland. London: Stephen Swift, 1912.
-     , Poetical Works. 2 vols. London: Macmillan, 1922.
Bonnerot, Louis, Matthew Arnold, poète: essai de biographie
     psychologique. Paris: M. Didier, 1947.
Boughton, L.N. and B.F. Stetler, A Concordance to the Poems
     of Robert Browning. 2 vols. New York: Stechert, 1924-25.
Brooks, Van Wyck, John Addington Symonds: A Biographical
     Study. London: Grant Richards, 1914.

Brown, E.K., "Matthew Arnold and the Elizabethans". University of Toronto Quarterly, 1 (1932), 333-51.
Brown, Horatio F., John Addington Symonds, A Biography. 2nd ed. London: Smith, Elder, 1903.
Browning, Robert, The Complete Works. Ed. Charlotte Porter and Helen A. Clarke, Vol. XII. New York: George D. Sproul, 1899.
‒ , The Complete Works. Ed. Roma A. King, et al. Vol. I. Athens: Ohio Univ. Press, 1969.
‒ , Letters of Robert Browning, Collected by Thomas J. Wise. Ed. T.L. Hood. New Haven: Yale Univ. Press, 1933.
‒ , New Poems by Robert Browning and Elizabeth Barrett Browning. Ed. Sir Frederic G. Kenyon. New York: Macmillan, 1915.
‒ , Robert Browning and Julia Wedgwood: A Broken Friendship as Revealed by Their Letters. Ed. Richard Curle. New York: Stokes, 1937.
‒ , The Works. Centenary Edition. 10 vols. Ed. F.G. Kenyon. London: Smith, Elder, 1912.
Caine, T. Hall, Recollections of Dante Gabriel Rossetti. London: Elliott Stock, 1882.
Chislett, William, George Meredith: A Study and Appraisal. Boston: R.G. Badger, 1925.
Clough, Arthur Hugh, The Correspondence. 2 vols. Ed. Frederick L. Mulhauser. Oxford: Clarendon Press, 1957.
‒ , Selected Prose Works. Ed. Buckner B. Trawick. University: Univ. of Alabama Press, 1964.
Crosland, T.W.H., The English Sonnet, 1917; rpt. London: Martin Secker, 1926.
Culler, A. Dwight, Imaginative Reason: The Poetry of Matthew Arnold. New Haven: Yale Univ. Press, 1966.
De Vane, William C., A Browning Handbook. 2nd ed. New York: Appleton, 1955.
Doughty, Oswald, A Victorian Romantic: Dante Gabriel Rossetti. London: Muller, 1949.
Duffin, H.C., Amphibian: A Reconsideration of Browning, A Portrait. London: Bower & Bower, 1962.
‒ , Arnold the Poet. New York: Barnes & Noble, 1962.
Faverty, Frederic E., "Browning's Debt to Meredith in James Lee's Wife". Essays in American and English Literature Presented to Bruce Robert McElderry, Jr. Ed. Max F.

Schulz. Athens: Ohio Univ. Press, 1967.

Finch, Edith, Wilfrid Scawen Blunt, 1840-1922. London: Jonathan Cape, 1938.

Fleming, G.H., Rossetti and the Pre-Raphaelite Brotherhood. London: Rupert Hart-Davis, 1967.

Foster, E.M., Abinger Harvest. New York: Harcourt, 1936.

Friedman, Norman, "The Jangled Harp: Symbolic Structure in 'Modern Love'." Modern Language Quarterly, 18 (1957), 9-26.

Going, William T., "The Brothers Rossetti and Youth and Love". Papers on Language and Literature, 4 (1968), 334-35.

-     , "Gascoigne and the Term 'Sonnet Sequence'". Notes & Queries, 1 N.S. (1954), 189-91.

-     , "A Note on 'My Lady' of Modern Love". Modern Language Quarterly, 7 (1946), 311-14.

-     , "A Peacock Dinner: The Homage of Pound and Yeats to Wilfrid Scawen Blunt". Journal of Modern Literature, 1 (1971), 303-10.

-     , "The Term Sonnet Sequence". Modern Language Notes, 64 (1947), 400-02.

Gosse, Edmund, Critical Kit-Kats. London: Heinemann, 1896.

Griffin, W.H. and H.C. Minchin, The Life of Robert Browning. London: Methuen, 1938.

Grosskurth, Phyllis, The Woeful Victorian, A Biography of John Addington Symonds. New York: Holt, 1964.

Guerard, Albert Joseph, Robert Bridges: A Study of Traditionalism in Poetry. Cambridge, Mass.: Harvard Univ. Press, 1942.

Hammerton, J.A., George Meredith: His Life and Art in Anecdote and Criticism. London: Grant Richards, 1909.

Hardman, William, A Mid-Victorian Pepys: The Letters and Memoirs. Ed. S.M. Ellis. London: Cecil Palmer, 1924.

Hatcher, Harlan H., The Versification of Robert Browning. Columbus: Ohio State Univ. Press, 1928.

Havens, Raymond D., The Influence of Milton on English Poetry. Cambridge, Mass.: Harvard Univ. Press, 1922.

Kelvin, Norman, A Troubled Eden: Nature and Society in the Works of George Meredith. Stanford: Stanford Univ. Press, 1961.

King, Roma A., Jr., The Focusing Artifice: The Poetry of Robert Browning. Athens: Ohio Univ. Press, 1968.

Leavis, F.R., Education and the University. London: Chatto &

Windus, 1948.

Lee, Sidney, Elizabethan Sonnets. 2 vols. London: Constable, 1904.

—, King Edward VII: A Biography. 2 vols. London: Macmillan, 1925.

Lentzner, Karl, "Robert Browning's Sonettdichtung." Anglia, 9 (1899), 500-17.

Lewis, C. S., English Literature in the Sixteenth Century. Oxford: Clarendon Press, 1954.

Lindsay, Jack, George Meredith: His Life and Work. London: Bodley Head, 1956.

Lytton, The [Fourth] Earl, Wilfrid Scawen Blunt: A Memoir by His Grandson. London: Macdonald, 1961.

MacEachen, Dougald B., "Tennyson and the Sonnet." Victorian Newsletter, No. 14 [1958], 1-8.

Meredith, George, The Letters. 3 vols. Ed. C. L. Cline. London and New York: Clarendon Press, 1970.

—, The Letters: Collected and Edited by His Son. 2 vols. London: Scribner's, 1912.

—, The Poetical Works. Ed. G. M. Trevelyan. New York: Scribner's, 1912.

—, Selected Poems. Ed. Graham Hough. London: Oxford Univ. Press, 1962.

Mitchell, Charles Bradford, "The English Sonnet in the Seventeenth Century", Summaries of Theses. Cambridge, Mass.: Harvard Univ. Press, 1938.

Milton, John, The Complete Poems. Ed. F. A. Patterson. New York: Crofts, 1934.

Miyoshi, Masao, The Divided Self: A Perspective on the Literature of the Victorians. New York: New York Univ. Press, 1969.

Morrison, Theodore, "'Dover Beach' Revisited." Harper's, 180 (1940), 235-44.

Nicolson, Harold. Tennyson's Two Brothers. Cambridge: Univ. Press, 1947.

Priestly, J. B., George Meredith, English Men of Letters Series. New York: Macmillan, 1926.

Pritchett, V. S., George Meredith and English Comedy. New York: Random House, 1969.

Pyre, J. F. A., Formation of Tennyson's Style. Madison, Wisc.: Univ. of Wisconsin Studies in Language and Literature, 1921.

Rawnsley, H.D., Memories of Tennyson. Glasgow: MacLehose, 1920.

Reader, Willie D., "Stanza Form in Meredith's Modern Love." Victorian Newsletter, No. 38 (Fall, 1970), 26-7.

Reynolds, Paul Everett, "The English Sonnet Sequence, 1783-1845." Diss. Harvard, 1938.

Ross, Janet, The Fourth Generation. London: Constable, 1912.

Rossetti, Christina, New Poems. Ed. William Michael Rossetti. London: Macmillan, 1896.

-        , Poetical Works (with Memoir and Notes by William Michael Rossetti). London: Macmillan, 1904.

Rossetti, Dante Gabriel, Dante Gabriel Rossetti: His Family-Letters with a Memoir. 2 vols. Ed. William Michael Rossetti. London: Ellis, 1895.

-        , Poems, Ballads and Sonnets. Ed. Paull F. Baum. New York: Doubleday, 1937.

-        , Letters. 5 vols. Ed. Oswald Doughty and J.R. Wahl. Oxford: Clarendon Press, 1965-67.

-        , The Works. Ed. William Michael Rossetti. London: Ellis, 1911.

Rossetti, William Michael, Democratic Sonnets. 2 vols. London: Alston Rivers, 1907.

-        , Some Reminiscences. New York: Scribner's, 1906.

Saintsbury, George, Matthew Arnold. Modern English Writers' Series. Edinburgh: Blackwood, 1899.

Sanderlin, George, "The Influence of Milton and Wordsworth on the Early Victorian Sonnet". A Journal of English Literary History, 5 (1938), 225-51.

Sandstrom, Glenn, "'James Lee's Wife'—and Browning's". Victorian Poetry, 4 (1966), 259-70.

Sassoon, Siegfried, Meredith. New York: Viking, 1948.

Scott, Janet, Les Sonnets élisabéthains. Paris: Libraire Ancienne Honoré Champion, 1929.

Sencourt, R.E. [R.E. George Gordon], The Life of George Meredith. New York: Scribner's, 1929.

Sharp, William, Sonnets of This Century. London: Walter Scott, [1886].

-        , William Sharp (Fiona Macleod): A Memoir compiled by his wife, Elizabeth A. Sharp. New York: Duffield, 1910.

Sherman, Stuart Pratt, Arnold: How to Know Him. Indianapolis, Ind.: Bobbs-Merrill, 1917.

Smith, John Henry, Hiding the Skeleton: Imagery in Feverel and

Modern Love. Lincoln, Nebr.: Nebraska Wesleyan Univ. Press, 1966.

Stange, G. Robert, Matthew Arnold: The Poet as Humanist. Princeton: Princeton Univ. Press, 1967.

Stevenson, Lionel, The Ordeal of George Meredith: A Biography. New York: Scribner's, 1953.

Swinburne, Algernon Charles, The Best of Swinburne. Ed. Clyde K. Hyder and Lewis Chase. New York: Nelson, 1937.

Symonds, John Addington, Animi Figura. London: Smith, Elder, 1882.

- , The Letters. Vol I. Ed. Herbert Schueller and Robert Peters. Detroit: Wayne State Univ. Press, 1967.

- , Vagabunduli Libellus. London: Kegan Paul, 1884.

Symons, Arthur, "Sir William Watson". Forum 67 (1922), 485-98.

Taplin, Gardner B., The Life of Elizabeth Barrett Browning. New Haven: Yale Univ. Press, 1957.

Tennyson, Alfred, The Poems. Ed. Christopher Ricks. London: Longmans, 1969.

Tennyson, Charles, Poems of the Day and Year. London: John Lane, 1895.

- , A Hundred Sonnets of Charles Tennyson Turner. Ed. John Betjeman and Sir Charles Tennyson. London: Rupert Hart-Davis, 1960.

Tennyson, Sir Charles, Alfred Tennyson. New York: Macmillan, 1949.

Tinker, C.B. and H.F. Lowry, The Poetry of Matthew Arnold: A Commentary. London: Oxford Univ. Press, 1940.

Tomlinson, Charles, The Sonnet: Its Origin, Structure, and Place in Poetry. London: John Murray, 1874.

Wordsworth, William, The Letters of William and Dorothy Wordsworth: The Later Years. Ed. E. deSelincourt. 3 vols. Oxford: Clarendon Press, 1939.

Wright, Elizabeth Cox, "The Significance of the Image Patterns in Meredith's Modern Love." Victorian Newsletter No. 13 (Spring, 1958), 1-9.

Young, G.M., Victorian England, 1936; rpt. New York: Doubleday, 1954.